Who's Who in Chaucer

A selection of books by the same author

THE GEORGIAN AGE
THE STUART AGE
THE PLANTAGENET AGE
THE POET'S CRAFT
THE CRAFT OF PROSE
CLOSE READINGS
CURRENT LITERARY TERMS
WITCH, SPIRIT, DEVIL
NEW READING *(in fourteen books)*
NEW HORIZONS *(in ten books)*

Who's Who
in Chaucer

A. F. SCOTT

TAPLINGER PUBLISHING CO., INC.

NEW YORK

First published in the United States in 1974
by Taplinger Publishing Co., Inc.
New York, New York

Printed in Great Britain

Library of Congress Catalog Card Number: 74-7631
ISBN 0-8008-8265-2

Contents

Foreword

Geoffrey Chaucer was a voluminous writer about people. People not only amused him; he had an obvious *fondness* for them. So if he was tickled by their frequently farcical behaviour, he was also touched by their misfortunes, whether in the 'real' world of fourteenth-century actuality, as he himself observed it, or in the imagined world of 'olde bokes', than which nothing (he says) delighted him more, except going out on a May morning to see the daisies making their first appearance of the year, scattered among the grasses of his London garden, with its little arbour and newly cut turf benches.

His pages include a torrent of people imagined from his own observation or from his reading, and it is often hard to pick one's way understandingly among the names he drops. Who were Eclympasteyr, Cambiuskan, Beneit, Andromacha, Mynos, Proigne, John Gower? *Who's Who in Chaucer* will tell you in a moment. It introduces these figures alphabetically, one by one, to make easier reading for those who are taking their first steps in the exploration of Chaucer's populous world, by giving brief notes of factual information, sufficient to the context in which they occur, yet not overloaded with detail. *Who's Who in Chaucer* is essentially a book to help beginners to find their way about his enchanted world. It is especially helpful to those who do not happen to have an up-to-date complete edition of his works, with notes and a glossary to elucidate the wealth of his allusions and descriptions.

Many of his figures are famous enough and need no note—

Venus, Adam, the Minotaur, Helen of Troy, for instance. Yet it is interesting to compare what you know and think about (say) Cleopatra, with what Chaucer knew and thought about this famous female from antiquity: and then, with the help of *Who's Who*, to refresh your memory with the actual facts. Chaucer's feeling for people includes some very vivid nameless figures, who, alas, cannot therefore find their way into *Who's Who*, though they are so memorable as to deserve a name and a place:

> *Have ye nat seyn somtyme a pale face*
> *Among a prees of hym that hath be lad*
> *Toward his deeth, wher as hym gat no grace,*
> *And swich a colour in his face hath had*
> *Men myghte knowe his face that was bistad,*
> *Amonges alle the faces in that route?*
> *So stant Custance, and looketh hire aboute.*

This must surely have been some individual memory of Chaucer's life in London used poetically by him to give you the intensity of his heroine's predicament.

This sense of pathos and compassion are as keen as his sense of comedy and fun, untouched by malice, as it is, which seems to rise from some calm depth of equable loving-kindness towards us all; for Chaucer includes *us*, his readers, or hearers—he used to read his poems aloud to the Court of King Richard II—*as people*. His way of telling a story ropes us in, dips us in Chaucerian imagination, and welcomes us into his mainly sunlit, richly populated world, all friends together.

Where did all Chaucer's people come from? The great tap-roots of his imagination were mainly fed by the following: personal observation of an entirely new keenness in his contemporary world; the *Bible* and the *Apocrypha*, from every book in which he has borrowed something; most of the poetry of ancient Rome (especially Ovid); recent and contemporary French and Italian poetry, including Guillaume de Lorris, Jean de Meung, Dante, Boccaccio and Petrarch. So his range includes some three civilisations, Jewish, Latin, and the then upspringing civilisation of Christendom, of which he was destined to be so vigorous a part.

NEVILL COGHILL

Introduction

By following a thread, Theseus found his way out of the maze
in Crete, but Chaucer's characters are far more varied and
complex than any labyrinth. For the purposes of this book
it may help us to recognise them more easily by placing
some of them below in readily defined groups.

First, those splendid original creations: the Wife of Bath,
the Prioress, Friar, Parson and Summoner who, among many
other characters invented by this master of human comedy,
stand with the best in English literature. Then there are
those taken from the distinguished narrators of Chaucer's
own time and before, but made indisputably his own:
Criseyde, Pandarus, Troilus, Helen, Griselda, Palamon,
Arcite and more. Also, figures of Greek and Roman mythology, moving from Olympus to court life, to everyday life,
mixing legend with human action, yet never very remote
from the imagination of the medieval age. Finally, the
numerous real people from history: Greek, Latin, French,
Italian authors; the heroes of conquest, discovery, and rule;
and also priests, scholars, doctors, artists, dreamers and
saints. To make distinction somewhat easier in this book, the
names of these once-living people appear in bold type.

When Chaucer's characters such as the Doctor of Physic,
the Man of Law, Dorigen, Chantecleer and others give lists
or catalogues of people as parallel examples to enlarge and
strengthen their narrative or argument, the list will be given,
wherever possible, in that particular entry, and each person
named will be recorded in an individual entry as well. When
the same characters appear in more than one tale or work,

their different roles are described. When action in a short tale or work involves a number of people, these are often included both under the entry for the principal character and separately, under a cross-reference alphabetically placed. No attempt has been made to include every reference to every person mentioned in the works covered, but all references of importance have been listed. For complete listing, readers are referred to the *Concordance to the Complete Works of Chaucer* (J. S. P. Tatlock and A. G. Kennedy).

General arrangement, sources and spelling

This book falls into two parts, the first dealing with *The Canterbury Tales*, the second with five of the major poems, *Troilus and Criseyde*, *The Book of the Duchess*, *The House of Fame*, *The Parliament of Fowls* and *The Legend of Good Women*.

Each of the two parts ends with a separate section for the animals (or birds, or monsters) in the works, and a complete list of all characters' names in alphabetical order, tale by tale or work by work, followed by line references. The first line reference given applies to the first appearance of a named character in the prologue, tale, link or major poem, and corresponds to the numbering in the complete editions of Chaucer's works; very occasionally, a second line reference is given to indicate a character's further action in the work. The line references given *in brackets* are from the text numbering in editions of single works, for the benefit of those not using a complete edition.

For the character list of *The Canterbury Tales*, W. W. Skeat's arrangement has been used, consisting of *The Prologue* followed by the tales in the groups A to I. This preserves the continuity of introductions, prologues, tales, epilogue and envoy. For the character list of the major poems, alphabetical order has been followed.

The spelling of head-words throughout follows the text of W. W. Skeat and F. N. Robinson. Several spellings of some names are given when they appear with variation in the text. Where there are variants, these are arranged alphabetically: e.g., where both 'Diane' and 'Dyane', or 'Citherea' and 'Cytherea' occur, the entry will be positioned according to the 'i' rather than the 'y' spelling, with the variant listed (likewise, with 'Ester' and 'Hester'—the former will appear as the head-word). In the entries themselves, the more contemporary spelling of proper names is used for the convenience of the reader; thus, OMER will be referred to as Homer.

The quotations from Chaucer are set to the pattern of prose, with capital letters showing the beginning of each metrical line.

I wish to express my thanks to the late H. S. Bennett and G. G. Coulton, to whom I owe my first and lasting appreciation of Chaucer; and I offer my thanks also to Professor F. N. Robinson both for his standard edition and his indispensable Chaucerian scholarship.

A. F. Scott

PART ONE

Who's Who in *The Canterbury Tales*

PART ONE

Who's Who in the Caregiver Role

A

Abigayl: Abigail, whose good advice saved the life of her husband Nabal, is praised by January. *The Merchant's Tale*

Abraham: The Hebrew patriarch, 'an holy man', and yet, says the Wife of Bath, he 'hadde wyves mo than two', as did Jacob. *The Wife of Bath's Prologue*

ABSOLON: Absalon, a parish clerk, in love with Alison, the carpenter's wife. He sings love songs and plays a two-stringed fiddle. One dark night, at her window, he begs for a kiss. She sits unclothed on the sill, so that he kisses her bottom. In anger he fetches a hot coulter for revenge and pleads for another kiss. Nicholas, the lodger, presents *his* bottom instead, which is struck with the hot iron. *The Miller's Tale*

ACHALEOUS: Achelous, the river-god of this river in Greece, takes the form of a bull in a contest with Hercules. *The Monk's Tale*

ACHILLES: The bravest of the Greeks in the Trojan War, whose spear has the power both to kill and cure. *The Squire's Tale*

ADAM: The first man and his wife Eve eat the fruit of the forbidden tree, and are then 'out-cast to wo and peyne'. The Pardoner comments: 'O glotonye, on thee wel oghte us pleyne!' *The Pardoner's Tale*

The first man suffers, for he is driven out of high prosperity 'to labour, and to helle, and to meschaunce', according to the Monk. *The Monk's Tale*

ADOUN: Adonis, the son of Cinyras, King of Cyprus, and Myrrha. A handsome youth, he is beloved by Aphrodite, then mortally wounded by a wild boar. From his blood, it is said, the flower anemone grew. *The Knight's Tale*

ADRIANE: Ariadne, daughter of Minos, King of Crete. *Introduction to The Man of Law's Tale*

ALCESTE: Alcestis, the faithful wife of Admetus. *The Franklin's Tale*; *Introduction to The Man of Law's Tale*

ALCIONE: Alcyone or Halcyone, wife of Cëyx. *Introduction to The Man of Law's Tale*

ALEYN: Alan, a bible-clerk from Solar Hall, Cambridge, who beats and cheats out of payment a thieving miller, and seduces his daugher. *The Reeve's Tale*

ALGARSYF: The elder son of Cambuskan and Elpheta. *The Squire's Tale*

Alisaundre: Alexander the Great, 356–323 B.C., son of Philip II of Macedon. 'This wyde world, as in conclusioun, He wan by strengthe.' He defeated Darius and many more. 'The world was his, what sholde I more devyse?' He died of fever. The Monk says he was poisoned, again false fortune. *The Monk's Tale*

ALISON: The young wife of John, an old carpenter of Oxford. She makes love to Nicholas, the lodger, when John is in one of the tubs in the roof, fearing a flood. Absalon also loves her and cries for a kiss beneath the window. She boldly sits unclothed on the sill to quieten him, and receives a misdirected kiss. *The Miller's Tale*

ALISOUN: The Wife of Bath's intimate friend, whose lodger John, a clerk of Oxford, becomes the Wife of Bath's fifth husband. *The Wife of Bath's Prologue*

ALLA: King of Northumberland. *The Man of Law's Tale*

Almache, Almachius: A Roman prefect who condemned to death for their Christian faith Cecilia, her husband Valerian, Tiburtius, and Maximus, a Roman officer. *The Second Nun's Tale*

Alocen: Alhazen, an Arabian mathematician of the 11th century, famous for his discoveries in optics. *The Squire's Tale*

ALYS, DAME: The Wife of Bath. *The Wife of Bath's Prologue*

Ambrose: St. Ambrose (*c.* A.D. 340–97), Bishop of Milan, one of the Fathers of the Church. *The Parson's Tale*

AMPHIORAX: Amphiaraus, in Greek mythology an Argive hero and a seer. He married Eriphyle, who persuaded him to become one of the Seven against Thebes. *The Wife of Bath's Prologue*

AMPHIOUN: Amphion, King of Thebes and husband of Niobe. He is a skilful harpist, and the stones of the walls of Thebes are drawn into place by his music. *The Manciple's Tale; The Knight's Tale*

ANDROMACHA: Andromache, the wife of Hector, who dreamed, the very night before, that her husband would be killed in battle. Chanticleer therefore tells Pertelote one should not ignore dreams. *The Nun's Priest's Tale*

ANTHEUS: Antaeus, the giant wrestler who is killed by Hercules. *The Monk's Tale*

ANTIOCHUS: Antiochus Epiphanes, King of Syria from 175 to 163 B.C. He raped his own daughter. His fierce attempt

5

to destroy the Jews was met by the heroic resistance of the Maccabees. He died in a state of raving madness. *Introduction* to *The Man of Law's Tale; The Monk's Tale*

Antonius: Antoninus, or Caracalla, Emperor of Rome, A.D. 211–17. He was murdered at Edessa by Macrinus, the praetorian prefect. *The Knight's Tale*

Apelles: The great Greek painter of the first half of the 4th century B.C., and favourite painter of Alexander the Great. *The Physician's Tale*

APIUS: Appius, a wicked judge who wants Virginia for himself. He suborns Claudius, a servant, to claim that she was stolen as a child. In court Appius rules that she should be his ward first of all. Virginia chooses death rather than shame. Her father cuts off her head, which he sends to the judge in court. The people throw Appius into prison, where he kills himself. *The Physician's Tale*

Apostle: St. Paul, who said in Ephesians 5: 25, 'Husbands, love your wives'. The Wife of Bath remarks, 'Al this sentence me lyketh every-deel'. *The Wife of Bath's Prologue*

APPOLLONIUS: The 'hero' of the romance *Apollonius of Tyre*, a tale of incest by an unknown Greek author, related by Chaucer's friend John Gower in his *Confessio Amantis*. *Introduction* to *The Man of Law's Tale*

ARCITA: Arcite is Palamon's cousin, and they are imprisoned by Theseus after the sack of Thebes. They see Emily in the garden and both fall in love with her. Arcite is released through the intercession of Perotheus, a friend of Theseus, and leaves Athens. In despair he takes the name of Philostrate and returns as a page in the house of Emily who pretends not to know that he loves her. He moves to the court of Theseus and rises in position. Palamon escapes from prison and meets Arcite in a field. They fight a duel, the winner to woo Emily; Theseus stops it and arranges

6

instead a tournament. Arcite with his knights captures Palamon and is declared the winner, but his horse stumbles (the work of the gods Pluto and Saturn) and he dies. (Palamon marries Emily.) *The Knight's Tale*

ARGUS: Argos Panoptes, in Greek legend the herdsman with a hundred eyes, known as the All-Seeing. *The Knight's Tale*

The Wife of Bath chides one of her husbands should he wish such a man to watch over her. *The Wife of Bath's Prologue*

Aristoclides: The tyrant of Orchomenos, two cities of ancient Greece. *The Franklin's Tale*

Aristotle: The great Greek philosopher, 384–322 B.C. His works on metaphysics, poetry, ethics, politics, logic and rhetoric had immense influence on medieval thought. All Oxford curricula included his work. The Clerk had 'twenty bokes, clad in blak or reed, Of Aristotle and his philosophye'. *The Prologue*

Arnold of the Newe Toun: Arnaldus de Villanova, or Arnaud de Villeneuve, 13th-century author of the *Philosopher's Rosary* on alchemy. *The Canon's Yeoman's Tale*

ARPIES, ARPIIS: The Harpies, mythical monsters with women's faces and vultures' bodies. In one of his Twelve Labours, Hercules slew 'the cruel briddes'. *The Monk's Tale*

ARRIUS: A character in the *Epistola Valerii*, a satirical miscellany of Walter Map, archdeacon of Oxford under Henry II. *The Wife of Bath's Prologue*

Arthemisie: Artemisia of Caria, a virtuous wife, who built the Mausoleum to the memory of her husband Mausolus, and was, as Dorigen says, 'Honoured . . . thurgh al the Barbarye'. *The Franklin's Tale*

7

ARTHOUR, ARTOUR: Arthur, King of Britain, a most romantic figure. According to legend, elves danced at his birth, and his sword and spear were of magic origin. As Chaucer says, 'Al was this land fulfild of fayerye'. *The Wife of Bath's Tale*

ARVERAGUS: The honourable knight in Brittany who marries Dorigen. Later she is bound by a promise to Aurelius to become his lover upon a seemingly impossible condition: to remove the rocks from the coast of Brittany. This is done, and Arveragus says the promise must be fulfilled, but Aurelius releases her from it. *The Franklin's Tale*

Assuer, Assuerus: Ahasuerus, the Persian King, husband of Esther. *The Merchant's Tale*

ATHALANTE: Atalanta, daughter of Iasus and Clymene, famous for her swiftness in foot-races. She will only marry a man who can outdistance her. She appears in a wall-painting in the Temple of Diana hunting the wild boar. *The Knight's Tale*

ATTHEON: Actaeon, the son of Aristaeus and Autonoe, was transformed into a stag by Diana, the goddess of chastity, when he by chance saw her bathing. He was later torn to pieces by his own hounds. *The Knight's Tale*

Attilla: Attila the Hun ravaged the Eastern Empire, A.D. 445–50. The Pardoner tells us he died in his sleep 'bledinge ay at his nose in dronkenesse'. *The Pardoner's Tale*

Augustyn, Austyn: St. Augustine (A.D. 354–430), Bishop of Hippo in Africa. This 'hooly doctour' was an authority on the subject of predestination and divine prescience. *The Prologue; The Nun's Priest's Tale*

Aurelian: Roman emperor (A.D. 270–75). *The Monk's Tale*

AURELIUS: A squire in Brittany in love with Dorigen, the wife of Arveragus. She makes her consent to his wish that he become her lover depend on the rocks of Brittany's coast being removed. This is done by a magician. Arveragus says she must fulfil her promise. On hearing this, Aurelius releases her. *The Franklin's Tale*

Averrois: A famous Arabian philosopher and medical authority (1126–98). He translated Aristotle, founded a philosophy of religion, and wrote a 'medical system' known as *Colliget* in the Latin translation. *The Prologue*

Avycen: Avicenna (930–1037), Arabian physician and philosopher, author of the *Canon of Medicine* which has a chapter on poisons. *The Prologue; The Pardoner's Tale*

B

BACHELER: A young knight of King Arthur's court sees a young woman walking alone, ravishes her, and is condemned to die. The queen and her ladies 'preyeden the king of grace', and so the knight is given the chance to save his life, by answering correctly within one year the question: 'What do women love most?' On condition that he does whatever she asks, a foul old woman tells him the answer: 'sovereyntee As wel over hir housbond as hir love.' By will of the royal court, and much against his desire, he has to marry her. Then she gives him a choice: to have her foul and old but true, or young, fair, and possibly unfaithful. The knight, in distress, says the choice is hers, and admits she has the mastery. Suddenly he sees her restored to youth and beauty, and they live in perfect joy. *The Wife of Bath's Tale*

BACUS: Bacchus, the god of wine. *Prologue* to *The Manciple's Tale*

9

BAILLY, Herry: *see* Hooste

Balthasar: Belshazzar, the son of Nebuchadnezzar, whose doom was foretold by the words *'Mene, Tekel, Peres'* on the wall during a great feast. They were interpreted by Daniel as a prophecy of immediate disaster. That night Belshazzar was slain, and Babylonia taken by the Medes and Persians. The Monk declares that there is no lordship that is secure. *The Monk's Tale*

Barnabo: Bernabò, Viscount of Milan. He was treacherously arrested by Gian Galeazzo in May 1385. In December of that year he died suddenly in prison. Chaucer knew him, having been on an embassy to Milan in 1378. He may well have written this stanza as soon as the sad news reached England.

[F. N. Robinson: 'Bernabò . . . was a character of special interest to Chaucer and the English court. His niece, Violanta, married Lionel Duke of Clarence; Bernabò had offered one daughter, Katerina, to Richard II, and had married another, Donnina, to Sir John Hawkwood.'] *The Monk's Tale*

Benedight, Beneit: St. Benedict, *c.* A.D. 480–544, established monasticism in Europe in 529 when he founded the monastery on Monte Cassino in Campania. The Rule of St. Benedict demanded poverty, chastity and obedience. *The Prologue; The Miller's Tale*

Bernard: Bernard Gordon, A Scot, was professor of medicine at Montpellier about 1300. *The Prologue*

St. Bernard (1091–1153), a great French priest, founded the abbey of Clairvaux, and dominated the Cistercian Order. *The Second Nun's Prologue*

BEVES: Sir Bevis of Hampton. *The Tale of Sir Thopas*

Bilyea: Bilia, the virtuous wife of Duillius. *The Franklin's Tale*

Boece: Boethius (A.D. 470–525), Toman statesman and philosopher, trusted adviser of Theodoric, King of the Ostrogoths, who ordered his death in 525. Chaucer translated his great work *De Consolatione Philosophiae*, part of which deals with predestination and free will, and was much influenced by it. He was regarded in the Middle Ages as a supreme musician. *The Nun's Priest's Tale*

Bradwardyn: Thomas Bradwardine, lecturer at Oxford and Archbishop of Canterbury at his death in 1349; he was author of a treatise *De Causa Dei* dealing with the problems of pre-ordination and free will. Chaucer mentions Boethius as well and illustrates the distinction between 'simple necessity' (God foreknows and fore-ordains all things) and 'conditional necessity' (God foreknows, but free choice is left to man). *The Nun's Priest's Tale*

BRITON CLERK: The magician who at Aurelius's request spirits away the rocks on the Brittany coast for a thousand pounds. This done, Dorigen must fulfil her promise to become Aurelius's lover. Her husband insists she should do so, but Aurelius releases her from her promise, and the magician refuses any payment. *The Franklin's Tale*

BRIXSEYDE: Briseis, a slave-girl belonging to Achilles. *Introduction* to *The Man of Law's Tale*

Brutus Cassius: Chaucer thought that Brutus and Cassius, the two chief assassins of Caesar, were one and the same person. *The Monk's Tale*

BUSIRUS: Busiris, King of Egypt, slain by Hercules. *The Monk's Tale*

C

CADME: Cadmus of Thebes, husband of Harmonia. He killed a dragon, sowed its teeth in the ground, and from each sprang an armed man. These warriors fought and all were killed except five, who were the ancestors of the Thebans. Arcite declares he is of that line. *The Knight's Tale*

CALISTOPEE, CALYXTE: Callisto, an Arcadian nymph, the daughter of Lycaon; she is changed into a bear by Diana, then to a star. On the wall of Diana's temple 'thus was it peynt'. *The Knight's Tale*

CAMBALO: The younger son of Cambuskan and Elpheta *The Squire's Tale*

CAMBIUSKAN, CAMBYUSKAN: Cambuskan, a king at Tzarev in Tartary, who could be Genghis Khan, or his grandson Kublai Khan. Elpheta is his wife; they have two sons Algarsyf and Cambalo, and a daughter Canace. Gawain comes with gifts from his lord, the King of India and Araby: a brass horse, the fastest flying creature; a mirror which can reveal everything past or future; a ring which brings understanding of the language of birds; a sword which can kill any beast, or cut through rock. The ring is given to Canace who hears the sad story of a female hawk. *The Squire's Tale*

CAMPANEUS: Capaneus, one of the Seven against Thebes. Zeus kills him with a thunderbolt as he scales the walls. *The Knight's Tale*

CANACE: The daughter and youngest child of Cambuskan and Elpheta. The King, her father, gives her Gawain's gift of a ring which brings understanding of the language of birds. She hears the sad story of a female falcon deserted by a tercelet falcon for a kite: 'he loved this kyte so, That al his love is cleve fro me ago.' Canace, with deep feeling, nurses the poor bird. *The Squire's Tale*

CANACEE: Canace is mentioned when the Man of Law condemns tales of incest and says of Chaucer, 'certeinly no word ne wryteth he Of thilke wikke ensample of Canacee, That lovede hir owne brother sinfully'. *Introduction* to *The Man of Law's Prologue*

CARTER: His cart full of hay becomes stuck in the mud. A summoner and yeoman (really a fiend) watch. The carter shouts, 'The devel have al, bothe hors and cart and hey!' As he does not mean it, the fiend will not take them. Soon the three horses pull the cart forward. *The Friar's Tale*

CATOUN: The *Disticha Catonis*, a 4th-century collection of moral sayings, are attributed to Dionysius Cato, and were used as a school book to teach Latin. When Pertelote says, 'Ne do no fors of dremes' (attach no importance to dreams), she is referring to the passage beginning *'Somnia ne cures . . .'* in Book ii, distich 32. *The Nun's Priest's Tale; The Miller's Tale;* also mentioned in *The Canon's Yeoman's Prologue*

CECILE, CECILIE: Cecilia, a noble Christian maiden in pagan Rome, tells her husband, Valerian, on their marriage night that her guardian angel protects her both waking and sleeping. If Valerian touches her, the angel will kill him. Valerian goes to Pope Urban, sees the angel and is himself baptised. The angel converts his brother Tiburtius too. The brothers are later commanded by the Roman prefect Almachius to make a sacrifice to Jupiter, but they refuse and are beheaded. Cecilia is also tried by Almachius, speaks bravely for Christ, and is sentenced to death. After 'three strokes in the nekke' she lives three days, preaching the faith. Urban buries her among his saints. Her house becomes the Church of St. Cecilia. (St. Cecilia died in Sicily in A.D. 176.) *The Second Nun's Prologue* and *Tale*

Cenobia, Cenobie: Zenobia, widow and successor in A.D. 266 of Odenathus, ruler of Palmyra, a city state in Syria under protection of Roman emperors. She was ambitious and invaded Asia Minor and Egypt in defiance of Rome. In 273 she was defeated by the emperor Aurelian, who led her in triumph in Rome. Her life was spared, and she lived in comfort with her sons at Tibur. *The Monk's Tale*

CEYS, SEYS: Cëyx, husband of Alcyone. *Introduction* to *The Man of Law's Tale*

CHANON, CHANOUN: The canon lives in London and practises alchemy. He visits a priest, borrows a mark, and repays it in three days. He proceeds to dupe the priest by performing experiments before him with great effect, faking successful results, turning quicksilver and chalk into silver. Finally he sells the supposed secret to the priest for forty pounds and promptly disappears. *The Canon's Yeoman's Tale*

CHAPMAN: Merchant, vintner, from whom the Shipman had stolen wine at Bordeaux. *The Prologue*

Chaucer THE PILGRIM: He joins the pilgrims at the Tabard, and when he has spoken to them 'was of hir felawshipe anow'. He is enthusiastic, glad to be going on this pilgrimage. In the link after *The Prioress's Tale*, the Host describes him as plump, mild in manner, rather wistful, staring at the ground as if looking for a hare. 'He semeth elvish by his contenaunce, For un-to no wight dooth he daliaunce.' This Chaucer is anxious to please, and seeks not to offend by coarse speech. Feeling his way, he reveals some ignorance and incompetence, also uneasiness about his accurate use of sources. He admires most of the pilgrims for they are nearly all successful in whatever they set out to do. Obviously he is impressionable and generous in his comments. (Chaucer the poet was obviously different, having a profound knowledge of human beings: he deliberately

14

misrepresents himself in the *Tales*.) *The Prologue; Prologue* to *The Tale of Sir Thopas*

Christopher: An image of St. Christopher, a Christian martyr of the 3rd century. A patron saint of wayfarers. *The Prologue*

Cipioun: *see* Scipioun

CIRCES: Circe, a mythical sorceress, the daughter of Helios and Perse, who charmed Ulysses and transformed his companions into swine on the island of Aiaie. *The Knight's Tale*

CITHEREA: Cytherea, *see* Venus

CLAUDIUS: A servant who, prompted by the judge Appius, makes the false claim that Virginia was stolen from him as a child. *The Physician's Tale*

CLERGEON, CLERGEOUN: A widow's choir-boy son, seven years old, he lives in a Christian town in Asia. He is murdered by the Jews because he sings '*O alma redemptoris mater*' when passing through the ghetto on his way to school. His body is thrown in a pit, but he is found by his mother and Christian people because he continues to sing though his throat is cut. The Virgin Mary has placed upon his tongue a grain of pearl, and when this is removed he 'yaf up the goost ful softely'. *The Prioress's Tale*

CLERK: He is a dedicated, unworldly scholar at Oxford, destined for a career in the church. He is poor, 'loked holwe, and ther-to soberly', speaks little but what is 'ful of hy sentence'. What little money he gets from his friends he spends on books. A truly good person, he lives an austere life: 'Gladly wolde he lerne and gladly teche.' *The Prologue*

An Oxford student, versed in logic and other studies. In the prologue of his own tale he says he has been to Padua, possibly to the University there. *Prologue* to *The Clerk's Tale*

CLITEMISTRA, CLITERMYSTRA: Clytemnestra, daughter of Tyndareus, King of Sparta, and wife of Agamemnon, King of Argos. She, with her lover Aegisthus, murdered her husband, and was slain by Orestes, Agamemnon's son. *The Wife of Bath's Prologue*

CONSTABLE: Governor of the castle on the Northumberland coast who rescues Constance from the shipwreck and, with Hermengild his wife, looks after her. Satan fills a young knight with desire for Constance, who will not yield, so he kills Hermengild with a knife and leaves it beside Constance's bed. The Governor returns with King Alla. Constance is tried for the murder. The knight is swearing her guilt when a hand appears which strikes him dead, and a voice is heard declaring her innocence. Then King Alla marries 'this holy mayden'. *The Man of Law's Tale*

Constantyn: Constantinus After, a Benedictine monk of Carthage, brought Arabian learning to Salerno in the 11th century and helped to found the medical school there. *The Prologue*

Referred to as 'the cursed monk daun Constantyn', he numbers many drugs in his book *De Coitu. The Merchant's Tale*

COOK: Roger the London cook accompanies the five gildsmen 'to boille the chiknes with the marybones'. He is master of his trade. Unfortunately he has a dry-scabbed ulcer on his shin, and is a drunkard. He is called Hodge of Ware. *The Prologue*

COUNTESSE OF PANIK: Walter's sister, who on her marriage lives in Bologna. *The Clerk's Tale*

CREON: The son of Menoeceus and brother of Jocasta. He became the tyrant of Thebes. *The Knight's Tale*

Cresus: Croesus the last King of Lydia, who reigned from 560 to 546 B.C., and who was rumoured to be the richest

16

man in the then known world. Conquered by the Persian Cyrus, he was led out to be burnt, but heavy rain fell and he escaped. He dreamt he was in a tree, with Jupiter to wash him and Phoebus to dry. His daughter Phanýa explained the dream: the tree was a gibbet, Jupiter the rain, Phoebus the sun. Croesus was hanged, says the Monk, and concludes: '. . . fortune alwey wol assaille With unwar strook the regnes that ben proude.' *The Monk's Tale;* also in *The Nun's Priest's Tale* and *The Knight's Tale*

CRISIPPUS: Chrysippus, probably the person mentioned by St. Jerome in his *Epistola Adversus Govinianum* and named by the Wife of Bath when speaking of the reading matter of her fifth husband, John. *The Wife of Bath's Prologue*

Crist: The Wife of Bath says Christ only went once to grace a wedding, that at Cana in Galilee. He also rebuked the Samaritan woman with the admonishment, 'Thou hast y-had fyve housbondes', and then claimed the last man was not her husband. The Wife of Bath, justifying her own five husbands, asks why one should not marry two or even eight. *The Wife of Bath's Prologue*

'Hym that harwed helle' is Christ, who descended into Hell and led Adam, Eve, St. John the Baptist and others to freedom. The harrowing of Hell was a common topic in the Christian literature and miracle plays of the Middle Ages. *The Miller's Tale*

CUSTANCE: Constance is daughter of a Christian Emperor in Rome. To marry her, a Syrian Sultan is baptised. The Mohammedans, led by his wicked mother-in-law, murder the Sultan and his fellow converts at the marriage feast in Syria. Constance, cast adrift, miraculously reaches Northumberland. After being falsely accused of murder, she marries King Alla, who is also converted. They have a son, Maurice. Alla's mother plots Constance's downfall, and soon she is again cast adrift, with the child, and by good fortune she reaches Rome. Alla sets out for Rome in penance, recognises his son and is happily reunited with Constance. They return to Northumberland. When Alla dies, Constance and her son return to Rome, where Maurice becomes Emperor. *The Man of Law's Tale*

Cutberd: St. Cuthbert, Bishop of Lindisfarne (*d.* A.D. 686). John, the student (with his friend Alan), invokes this saint when asking Simon the miller for hospitality. *The Reeve's Tale*

D

Dalida: Delilah was beloved by Samson, but she betrayed him to the Philistines by persuading him to divulge the secret of his strength—his hair. Once shorn of it he is overcome. *The Monk's Tale*

Damascien: Possibly Johannes Damascenus, an Arabian physician and theologian of the 9th century A.D. *The Prologue*

DAMYAN: Damian falls in love with May, the young wife of the stupid old rake January, who goes blind. In the garden, Damian and May take advantage of his blindness in a pear-tree, but suddenly Pluto restores January's sight and he shouts in anger at what he sees. Proserpine provides May's excuse that January's sight is still imperfect and he has only witnessed May struggling with a man in a tree. He accepts this, and in happiness 'clippeth hir ful ofte'. *The Merchant's Tale*

DANE: Daphne, who, fleeing from the embraces of Apollo,

cried to the gods for help. They turned her into a laurel tree. *The Knight's Tale*

Daniel: Chanticleer asks Pertelote if Daniel in the Old Testament 'held dremes any vanitee'. *The Nun's Priest's Tale*

Dant: Dante Alighieri (1265–1321), the great Italian epic poet, author of *La Divina Commedia. The Monk's Tale*

DAUN JOHN: Sir John, a monk, friend of a rich, mean merchant in St. Denys, whose beautiful wife asks him to lend a hundred francs to buy finery. To buy some cattle, John borrows the sum from the merchant, who leaves for Bruges. Then John, in exchange for that money, makes love to the merchant's wife; he later tells the merchant he has repaid the loan. The wife is blamed for not telling her husband this, and explains that she has used the money to buy new clothes. *The Shipman's Tale*

DAUN PIERS: Peter or Pierce. This is the name given by the Host to the Monk after his tale, 'sir Monk, or daun Piers by your name'. *The Nun's Priest's Prologue*

David: The second King of Israel. To him are attributed the Book of Psalms of the Old Testament, which were the unchallenged basis of medieval church services. *The Manciple's Tale*

DEETH: Death, coming into the tale as a 'privee theef', kills a friend of three rioters, who then set out to find him. *The Pardoner's Tale*

DEMOCIONES DOGHTER: The daughter of Demotion, when she hears of the death of the man she was to marry, kills herself to avoid having to marry another. *The Franklin's Tale*

DEMOPHON: The betrothed of Phyllis. *Introduction* to *The Man of Law's Tale*

Deyscorides: Dioscorides, a Greek physician of the 2nd century A.D. His *Materia Medica*, in five books, deals at great length with medicinal herbs. *The Prologue*

DIANE: Diana, the Roman goddess identified with the Greek Artemis. She was the daughter of Zeus and Leto and twin sister of Apollo. Goddess both of chastity and of hunting, she is also associated with the moon, and was believed to have the powers of Proserpina in the underworld. Emily's words, 'Now help me, lady, sith ye may and can, For tho thre formes that thou hast in thee', refer to the goddess as the Moon in Heaven, as Diana on earth, and as Proserpina in Hell. *The Knight's Tale*

DIANIRA, DIANIRE: Dejanira, wife of Hercules, shot Nessus, a centaur, with a poisoned arrow in self-defence. As he lay dying, Nessus told her to keep some of his blood which, smeared on a garment, would keep Hercules' love for ever. Hercules fell in love with Iole; Dejanira sent him a robe dipped in the blood, which made Hercules suffer fearfully. To escape from it he was carried up Mount Oeta and placed on a pyre which was quickly set alight. *The Wife of Bath's Prologue*

DIDO: Queen of Carthage. *Introduction* to *The Man of Law's Tale*

DIVES: The rich man in the parable. *The Summoner's Tale*

DOCTOUR OF PHISIK: The Doctor, or Physician, being richly dressed, gives the impression of affluence, though he is cautious about food and slow in spending money. He is a distinguished member of his profession. By knowledge of 'natural magic' he chooses for his patient astrological hours that would help the treatment, and the right time for making talismanic effigies. He knows which 'humour' has caused the illness, and all the authorities in medicine: Esculapius, Descorides, Rufus, Ypocras, Haly, Galyen,

Serapion, Razis, Avycen, Averrois, Damascien, Constantyn, Bernard, Gatesden, and Gilbertyn. *The Prologue*

DONEGILD: The mother of Alla, King of Northumberland, who writes false letters to destroy his marriage to Constance, saying their son has been born horribly disfigured, and later that the King has commanded that his wife and son should be thrust out to sea. Alla returns from the wars, discovers what has been done, and Donegild is put to death. *The Man of Law's Tale*

DORIGEN: The wife of Arveragus. Both are brave and honourable. A squire, Aurelius, is in love with Dorigen. To escape from his attentions she makes her consent depend upon an impossible achievement, that he should remove all the rocks on the Brittany coast. A student of magic accomplishes this for Aurelius, who tells her that her condition has been met. In a moving speech, the distressed Dorigen gives a list of virtuous women: Stymphalis, Lucrece, Alcestis, Penelope, Laodamia, Portia, Artemisia, Teuta, Bilia, Valeria and Rhodogoun. When she tells her husband of her promise, he says she must fulfil it. When Aurelius knows of this, in generous spirit he releases her from that promise. *The Franklin's Tale*

Dunstan, Seint: St. Dunstan (A.D. 909–88), the famous abbot of Glastonbury and Archbishop of Canterbury, who lived through seven reigns from Athelstan to Ethelred, and displayed great political influence. *The Friar's Tale*

E

ECTOR: Hector, son of King Priam of Troy. *The Nun's Priest's Tale*

EGEUS: Aegeus, father of Theseus—*The Knight's Tale*

Egipcien Marie: St. Mary of Egypt of the 5th century. After a youth of wantonness she was converted, and then lived for forty-seven years in the desert beyond Jordan. *The Man of Law's Tale*

Eleyne: Helena, the mother of the Emperor Constantine, was converted to Christianity by her son. It is believed she discovered the True Cross, for which she began searching after the Emperor's vision of a cross in the sky. She became St. Helen. *The Pardoner's Tale*

ELEYNE: Helen of Troy. *Introduction* to *The Man of Law's Tale*

Eliachim: Eliakin, a priest of Bethulia, a city of the Israelites besieged by Holofernes. *The Monk's Tale*

ELPHETA: The wife of Cambuskan. *The Squire's Tale*

EMELYA, EMELYE: Emily is the sister of Hippolyta and the sister-in-law of Theseus, Duke of Athens. Palamon and Arcite, cousins of noble Theban families, are imprisoned after the fall of Thebes, but are able to see Emily in the garden. They both fall in love with her. Emily does little but look beautiful—she is as 'fresshe' as May, to which she is frequently compared—sing and remain passive. When Arcite becomes a servant in her house under the name 'Philostrate' she recognises him, but pretends not to know that he loves her. Later, when a tournament is planned to decide who shall marry her, she prays to Diana that she may remain chaste. However, when Arcite is acclaimed winner of the tournament against Palamon she is overjoyed: 'she agayn him caste a freendlich yë, (For wommen, as to speken in comune, They folwen al the favour of fortune).' But after falling from his horse, Arcite dies. When a period of mourning has elapsed, Emily gladly marries Palamon, with the blessing of Theseus. *The Knight's Tale*

EMETRIUS: King of the Indians. *The Knight's Tale*

EMPEROUR OF ROME: The father of Constance. *The Man of Law's Tale*

ENEE, ENYAS: Aeneas, of the royal family of Troy, leaves the burning city with a fleet. Shipwrecked near Carthage, he is welcomed by Dido, who falls in love with him. When he deserts her, she takes her own life. *Introduction* to *The Man of Law's Prologue*

Epicurus: Greek philosopher (341–270 B.C.), who taught that the highest good was the practice of virtue. He came to be regarded as the patron of refined sensuous enjoyment, and in this sense the Franklin 'was Epicurus owene sone'. *The Prologue*

ERCULES: Hercules, the strongest of men, slays the Harpies (winged monsters); drives Cerberus, the guardian dog, from Hell; kills Busiris, the tyrant-king of Egypt; slays Cacus the giant and Antaeus the giant wrestler; and overcomes Achelous, the river-god in the form of a bull. He dies from a tunic or shirt poisoned by the blood of Nessus, the centaur. *The Monk's Tale; The Knight's Tale*

ERL OF PANIK: Lord Panaro of Bologna, the husband of Walter's sister, on whose estate the two offspring of Walter and Griselda are reared. *The Clerk's Tale*

ERRO: Hero, in Greek legend the priestess of Venus in Sestos, beloved by Leander who drowned swimming the Hellespont to visit her. *Introduction* to *The Man of Law's Tale*

ESCULAPIUS: Aesculapius, in Greek mythology the son of Apollo and Coronis. He is said to have learnt the art of medicine from the wise centaur Chiron, and was worshipped as the god of healing at his famous temple at Epidaurus. *The Prologue*

Ester, Hester: Esther helped God's people, and made her husband, Ahasuerus, promote Mordecai. She is praised by January. *The Merchant's Tale*

F

FELAWE: The hypocritical Friar John's companion. He carries a staff tipped with horn, a pair of ivory tablets and a stylus. The Friar records the names of those who give them food as if he will pray for them. *The Summoner's Tale*

FERMERER: A friar in charge of an infirmary. This man with his friend the sexton sees, through revelation (as does the friar telling the tale), the death of a baby and also 'saugh him born to blisse'. *The Summoner's Tale*

FRANKELEYN: The Franklin is a well-to-do landowner, but not of noble birth. Described as an epicure, he enjoys good food, wine, company, and keeps an open house. 'It shewed in his hous of mete and drinke, Of alle deyntees that men coude thinke.' He is an important figure—a Justice of the Peace, a Member of Parliament, and auditor of taxes. The other pilgrims seem to like him. *The Prologue*

FRERE: Hubert, the Friar, is a limiter: his begging for alms is limited to a certain district. A popular preacher, he gives easy penance to the rich. He helps the girls he has seduced to get married. His many activities, none of which accord with his vows of poverty, chastity and obedience, include peddling pins for curls and pocket-knives, frequenting taverns, and arbitrating in disputes, dressed impressively in 'his semi-cope, That rounded as a belle out of the presse'. He is hypocritical and cynical, scorning the poor and sick. Always covetous, he makes an abuse of the confession, persuading poor folk to give money for divine forgiveness. Venal and avaricious, he is termed 'the best beggere in his hous'. *The Prologue*

FRERE JOHN: At Holderness in Yorkshire this greedy, hypocritical friar goes about with a second friar and a sturdy rascal deluding simple villagers. The friar enters the house of the bedridden Thomas, embraces the wife, and asks to be left alone to discuss spiritual matters which turn on the sin of anger, mentioning Seneca, Cambyses and Cyrus. He asks Thomas for gold for the friars. The man says something 'hid in privetee'. When the friar gropes in the bed for it 'amydde his hand he leet the frere a fart'. After this insult, the servants leap in and chase the friar out. Jankin's solution for a share-out is an anti-climax for the friar. *The Summoner's Tale*

G

Galien, Galyen: Galen (*c.* A.D. 129–99) born at Pergamum in Mysia, was one of the most famous physicians of antiquity, a friend of Marcus Aurelius. He left a mass of medical writings, and over a hundred of these survive. Chaucer's doctor had read Galen. *The Prologue;* also mentioned in *The Parson's Tale*

Gatesden: John of Gaddesden of Merton College, Oxford, court physician under Edward II, wrote *Rosa Anglica*, a treatise on medicine. A thrifty man, perhaps Chaucer refers to him in the line: 'And yet he was but esy of dispence.' *The Prologue*

Gaufred, Gaufride: Geoffrey de Vinsauf, 12th-century poet on the art of Rhetoric. His passage on the plaintive style in *De Nova Poetria* begins with a description of the death of Richard I. Here, Chaucer gently ridicules him, saying he wished he had Geoffrey's style and skill to chide a Friday too, in reference to the fact that Richard received his fatal wound on a Friday. *The Nun's Priest's Tale*

GAWAYN, GAWEYN: Sir Gawain, a courteous and brave knight, nephew of King Arthur. During the celebrations at the court of King Cambuskan, Gawain arrives, bringing gifts from the King of India and Araby, his sovereign lord. *The Squire's Tale*

Genelloun, Genylo(u)n: Ganelon, the betrayer of Roland who was slain in the defeat of the rearguard of Charlemagne's army by the Moors at Roncesvalles. Chanticleer has no knowledge of the deceitful fox 'false mordrour, lurkynge in thy den'. *The Nun's Priest's Tale*

Ganelon's name is used as an adjective to distinguish a treacherous Genylon-Olyver 'corrupt for meede' from a Charles-Olyver 'that took ay heede Of trouthe and honour'. *The Monk's Tale*

GERVEYS: Gervase, the blacksmith who lends a hot coulter to Absalon, with which he strikes Nicholas's bare bottom sticking out of a window. *The Miller's Tale*

Gilbertyn: Gilbertus Anglicus, one of the thirteenth-century English writers on medicine; said to have been Chancellor at Montpellier. *The Prologue*

GO(D)DELIEF: The wife of the Host, Harry Bailey. When Chaucer's *Tale of Melibee* is over, the Host, speaking to the Monk, says he wishes his wife could have heard the tale: 'For she nis no-thing of swich pacience As was this Melibeus wyf Prudence.' *The Monk's Prologue*

GRISILDE, GRISILDIS: Griselda, the wife of Walter the marquis, is loyal, long-suffering and submissive. She is long separated from her two children, and returns to her old father, bearing all her suffering with patience. Walter recognises her qualities, brings her back and they live in happiness. Her daughter marries a lord; her son is to succeed to his father's heritage. *The Clerk's Tale*

GY: Sir Guy of Warwick. *The Tale of Sir Thopas*

H

HABRADATE: Abradates, King of the Susi. When he is slain, his wife kills herself. *The Franklin's Tale*

Haly: Probably the Persian Hali ibn el Abbas, a physician of the Eastern Caliphate who died A.D. 994. The name might also refer to Hali filius Rodbon. *The Prologue*

Hanybal: Hannibal (247–183 B.C.), the famous Carthaginian general who waged war against Rome. *The Man of Law's Tale*

HARLOT: A rascal who follows the greedy Friar John and his companion. He bears a sack for carrying whatever folk give them. *The Summoner's Tale*

Hasdrubales wyf: Hasdrubal was King of Carthage, defeated by Scipio Africanus Major in 146 B.C. He surrendered to save his life. His wife in anger threw herself and her sons into the flames of burning Carthage. (Chaucer thought the motive for her action was to escape from Roman villainy, however.) *The Nun's Priest's Tale; The Franklin's Tale*

Helowys: Heloïse, the wife of Abelard. *The Wife of Bath's Prologue*

HERMENGYLD: Hermengild, wife of the Constable of a

castle in Northumberland, who looks after Constance and becomes a Christian. A young knight, urged by Satan, murders her, and leaves the knife beside the bed of Constance, who would not yield to his desire. *The Man of Law's Tale*

Hermes: Hermes Trismegistus, said to be the author of many works on alchemy and magic. The Canon's Yeoman calls him the father of philosophy. *The Canon's Yeoman's Tale*

HERMYON: Hermione, daughter of Menelaus. *Introduction* to *The Man of Law's Tale*

Herodes: Herod, King of Judaea, 40–4 B.C. He was drunk, according to the Pardoner, when he ordered the death of John the Baptist. *The Pardoner's Tale; The Prioress's Tale*

HERRY BAILLY: *see* Hooste

Hester: *see* Ester

HOGGE OF WARE: The Cook says he 'highte Hogge of Ware'. Hodge is a nickname for Roger; Ware is in Hertfordshire, and Chaucer may be referring to a real person. *The Cook's Prologue* (*see* Cook)

HOOSTE: The Host, Harry Bailey (we learn his name from the Cook), landlord of the Tabard inn, is an imposing, congenial person, 'for to han been a marchal in an halle'. He suggests that on the journey to Canterbury each pilgrim should tell two tales going and two coming back, and on return the one whose tale is best shall have a supper, paid for by all, in the Tabard. The pilgrims accept his plan, beg him to be their Governor, the judge of the tales, and referee. The Host is a good listener, and bold in speech. Most polite to the Knight and Prioress, he handles the rough pilgrims well. He interrupts Chaucer's boring *Tale of Sir*

Thopas, decisively putting an end to it. He hints that Gode-lief, his wife, is shrewish, and their life together is not serene. Though he likes to appear plain, he quotes Seneca, can calculate date and time of day, and is always good company. *The Prologue*

HORN CHILDE: Hero of the romances King Horn, Horn Childe. *The Tale of Sir Thopas*

HUBERD: Hubert, *see* Frere

Hugelyn: Count Ugolino of Pisa, condemned by the lies of Bishop Ruggieri, was locked in prison with his three child-ren, all under five years of age, where all four starved to death. The Monk informs us that this tragic story is found in Dante. *The Monk's Tale*

Hugh of Lincoln: A Christian child alleged to have been crucified by a Jew named Copin or Joppin at Lincoln in 1255. The body is said to have been found in a well and buried in the cathedral after several miracles occurred. The Prioress prays to this English saint that God may send mercy down to mankind. *The Prioress's Tale*

Hym that harwed Helle: *see* Crist

I

ISIPHILEE: Hypsipyle, daughter of Thoas, was deserted by Jason. *Introduction* to *The Man of Law's Tale*

J

JANEKYN: The apprentice of the Wife of Bath and her husband. The wife disclaims any special interest in the handsome boy: 'For he squiereth me bothe I wol hym up and down, Yet hastow caught a fals suspecioun. I wol hym noght, thogh thou were deed tomorwe!' *The Wife of Bath's Prologue*

JANICULA: Griselda's father, who gives comfort in her severest testing time. When she returns to her husband, the marquis, her father also finds a safe place at his court. *The Clerk's Tale*

JANKIN: This squire of the lord of the manor listens with the family in the hall to the angry friar describing Thomas's action and the man's request of a certain sharing. Jankin then suggests that as a cartwheel has twelve spokes, twelve friars should lay their noses at each end with the churl at the centre, and this with sound and movement solves the problem of 'departynge of the fart on twelve'. *The Summoner's Tale*

A derisive name for a priest, who is often referred to as Sir John. *The Man of Law's Epilogue*. Also JENKIN. *The Shipman's Prologue*

JANUARIE: January, a prosperous knight in Pavia, Lombardy. At the age of sixty, after many years as a libertine, he decides to marry, citing examples of good women—Rebecca, Judith, Abigail, Esther—and quoting freely from Seneca, Cato and the Bible. He discusses the matter with his friends Placebo and Justinus. Soon he marries the young girl May. Damian falls in love with May. January goes blind. The wife and her lover take advantage of this and make love in a pear-tree, at which point Pluto, King of Faeryland, restores the husband's sight, but Proserpina enables May to outwit him, and they return to happiness. *The Merchant's Tale*

JANUS: Ancient Italian deity, the god of the doorway *(janua)*. He presides over the year, his special month being named January. As this month looks before and behind, he is represented in statues with two heads, both bearded, looking in opposite directions. *The Franklin's Tale*

JASON: In mythology, leader of the Argonauts. *Introduction to The Man of Law's Tale*

Jepte: Jephthah, son of Gilead, who overcame the Ammonites, after vowing to the Lord that, granted victory, he would offer as sacrifice whoever met him on return. His daughter met him, and was given two months' grace, in which she bewailed her virginity, before her death. (This story is an exemplar of the fate of Virginia.) *The Physician's Tale*

Jeremye: Jeremiah, the Hebrew prophet, who said 'thou shalt swere sooth thyne othes, and nat lye', is quoted by the Pardoner. *The Pardoner's Tale*

Jerome: St. Jerome, *c.* A.D. 340–420. He visited Gaul and Asia Minor, and later lived as a hermit near Chalcis on the frontier of Syria. He praised asceticism and condemned frivolous life. The fifth husband of the Wife of Bath read St. Jerome in one volume containing several works by various authors on the subject of 'wikked wyves'. She denounces such works. *The Wife of Bath's Prologue*

JEW: The man who murdered the seven-year-old chorister, and is eventually caught. They 'kitte his throte, and in a pit him caste'. *The Prioress's Tale*

Jhesus Syrak: Jesus, son of Sirach, the supposed author of *Ecclesiasticus. The Merchant's Tale; The Tale of Melibee*

Job: A man of wealth, suddenly overtaken by calamities, who showed patience under misfortune: 'Only the body and nat the soule greve.' *The Friar's Tale*

JOHN: A rich old carpenter in Oxford with a young wife, Alison. Nicholas, the lodger, persuades him to hang three tubs in the roof in preparation for an imminent flood. With John in the tub, he makes love to Alison. Later, hearing Nicholas's cry of 'water', John cuts the ropes and falls on the floor, breaking his arm. *The Miller's Tale*

A bible-clerk from Solar Hall, Cambridge, who deceives, humiliates and beats the thieving miller, and sleeps with his wife. *The Reeve's Tale*

Jonas: Jonah, when sailing for Tarshish, was thrown by sailors into the sea during a storm. He was swallowed by a great fish, but was eventually thrown up on shore. *The Man of Law's Tale*

Joseph: The son of Jacob who would certainly have known, as Chanticleer asserts, that dreams are a warning. *The Nun's Priest's Tale*

Jovinian: A monk and adversary of St. Jerome, who attacked him vigorously for his alleged worldliness. *The Wife of Bath's Prologue; The Summoner's Tale*

Judas: Judas Iscariot, who betrayed Christ for thirty pieces of silver. The Friar says that the summoner in his tale is just such a thief. *The Friar's Tale*

Judas Machabeus: Judas Maccabeus (d. 160 B.C.), leader of the Jews against Antiochus Epiphanes. *The Tale of Melibee*

Judith: She slew Holofernes while he slept and saved God's people wisely, and is therefore praised by January. *The Merchant's Tale; The Tale of Melibee*

Julian: St. Julian, patron of hospitality, said to have lived in the early 4th century. *The Prologue*

Julius, Gaius Julius: Julius Caesar (*c.* 101–44 B.C.), Roman general, statesman and emperor. 'Fro humble bed to royal magestee, Up roos he, Julius the conquerour.' He overcame Pompey, was triumphant in Rome, but a conspiracy by Brutus and other traitors led to his assassination. The Monk recommends the works of Lucan, Suetonius, and Valerius who wrote of these two conquerors, to whom fortune was first a friend and then a foe. *The Monk's Tale; The Knight's Tale*

JUNO: Wife of Jupiter, one of the great goddesses, worshipped as queen of heaven and identified with Hera. Her anger against Thebes was caused by Jupiter's love of Semele and Alcmena. *The Knight's Tale*

JUPITER: Roman god, king of heaven. *The Knight's Tale*

JUSTINUS: January's friend who advises him on his marriage to May. *The Merchant's Tale*

Juvenal: Decimus Junius Juvenalis (*c.* A.D. 60–130), the Roman satirical poet, who denounced the vices of the Rome of his day, and found an advantage in poverty: 'The povre man, whan he goth by the weye, Bifore the theves he may singe and pleye.' *The Wife of Bath's Tale*

K

Kenelm, Seint: Kenulphus, King of Mercia, died in
A.D. 821, leaving his son Kenelm, a child of seven, heir
to the throne. He was left to the care of his aunt, Quene-
dreda, who plotted his murder. Shortly before his death,
Kenelm dreamed that he climbed a tree; one of his friends
cut it down, and he flew to heaven in the shape of a bird.
Chanticleer refers to Kenelm. *The Nun's Priest's Tale*

KNYGHT: The Knight is the epitome of chivalry, a man of
distinction, integrity, and prudence: 'a verray, parfit gentil
knyght.' His campaigns have all been in defence of Christendom: to expel the Moors from Spain and North Africa; to
help King Peter of Cyprus in the Eastern Mediterranean;
to crusade in Eastern and Western Europe. Just back from
service, his campaigning dress, 'bismotered habergeoun',
shows that for him the pilgrimage to Canterbury is a religious one, not a social gathering for self-display. *The
Prologue*

L

LADOMYA, LAODOMEA: Laodamia, the faithful wife of
Protesilaus. *Introduction* to *The Man of Law's Tale; The
Franklin's Tale*

Lamek, Lameth: Lamech is mentioned in Genesis as the
husband of two wives, Adah and Zillah. *The Squire's Tale*

Lamuel: King Lemuel was told by his mother that it was
not for kings to drink wine, nor for princes to take strong

34

drink (Proverbs 31). The Pardoner mentions him during his condemnation of drunkenness. *The Pardoner's Tale*

LATUMIUS: Latumyus, a character in the *Epistola Valerii* of Walter Map, had three wives who hanged themselves from the same tree. *The Wife of Bath's Prologue*

LAUNCELOT: A knight of King Arthur's court and lover of Queen Guinevere. Well versed in court life, he could certainly describe such a scene as that taking place at King Cambuskan's court. *The Squire's Tale; The Nun's Priest's Tale*

Lazar: Lazarus. *The Summoner's Tale.*

LEANDRE: Leander of Abydos, lover of Hero. *Introduction* to *The Man of Law's Tale*

Looth: Lot, son of Haran, brother of Abraham. The Pardoner says he was drunk and 'nyste what he wroghte' when he 'lay by his doghtres two'. *The Pardoner's Tale*

Lord of Palatye: The Bey of Balat in Turkey, who though an infidel was allied by treaty to Peter of Cyprus. *The Prologue*

Loy, Seinte: St. Eligius, Bishop of Noyon, was famed for his beauty, his integrity and courtesy as well as for his artistic skill. His character corresponds to that of the Prioress herself. *The Prologue*

LUCINA: A title given to Juno and Diana in their capacity as goddesses of child-birth. *The Knight's Tale; The Franklin's Tale*

Lucrece, Lucresse: Lucretia, the faithful wife of L. Tarquinius Collatinus, who took her own life. *The Franklin's Tale; Introduction* to *The Man of Law's Tale*

Lucye: Lucia, Lucilia, the wife of the great Roman philosophical poet Lucretius, accidentally poisoned her husband with a love philtre, administered so that 'he sholde alwey up-on hir thinke'. *The Wife of Bath's Prologue*

LYBEUX: Hero of the romance *Libeaus Desconus*. *The Tale of Sir Thopas*

Lyma: An error for Livia or Livilla, wife of Drusus, the son of Tiberius. With the help of Sejanus she caused her husband to be poisoned. *The Wife of Bath's Prologue*

Lynyan: Giovanni da Lignaco (or Legnano), Professor of Law in Bologna, 1363. He wrote works on law, astrology and other learned arts. *The Clerk's Prologue*

M

MABELY: Mabel, an old widow, is visited by a summoner with a summons-bill and a threat of excommunication unless she pays him twelve pence. She refuses. He demands her new pan. A fiend disguised as a yeoman is present and hears her commend the summoner to the Devil, so he carries the blackguard off to hell. *The Friar's Tale*

Macrobes, Macrobeus, Macrobye: Macrobius, Latin author of the 5th century A.D., was not the writer but the commentator of *Somnium Scipionis* (Scipio's Dream), which formed the close of Cicero's lost treatise *De Republica*. In this tale, Pertelote is told of the importance of all dreams, Scipio's among them. *The Nun's Priest's Tale*

Mahoun, Makomete: Mahomet (A.D. 570–632), the founder of Islam, the religion of the Moslems. *The Man of Law's Tale*

MAIUS, MAY: May becomes the fresh young wife of the sanctimonious, elderly January, whose squire, Damian, falls in love with her. January goes blind. In the garden, at a sign from May, Damian climbs into a pear-tree. May, after mentioning her pregnancy and her craving for a pear to her husband, is helped by January into the tree where she and Damian make love, but though the watching Pluto restores January's sight, Pluto's wife Proserpina provides May with an excuse for her behaviour. *The Merchant's Tale*

MALKYN: The name is a diminutive of Matilda. She chases the fox 'with a dystaf in hir hand'. *The Nun's Priest's Tale*

MALYNE: Molly, the daughter of Simkin the miller. *The Reeve's Tale*

MARCHANT: The Merchant 'was ther with a forked berd'. Fashionably dressed, he talks always of his business success. Most of his trade is between England and the Netherlands. His 'chevisaunce' is a way of making money out of money, by lending at interest; the practice was considered a form of usury. Though so much is known about him, Chaucer adds: 'sooth to seyn, I noot how men him call.' *The Prologue*

MARCHANT AT SEINT DENYS: The rich but niggardly merchant lives in St. Denys with his beautiful wife. Among their guests, a young monk, Sir John, claims to be his cousin. The wife tells the monk her husband is 'in no degree the value of a flye', and asks John for the loan of a hundred francs to buy finery. Then the monk, ostensibly to buy some cattle, borrows a hundred francs from the merchant, who leaves for Bruges. Soon after, John returns to the house and in exchange for this money he and the wife make love. Later, at the abbey, the merchant visits the monk, who tells him he has paid the borrowed money to his wife. The merchant chides his wife for not telling him the loan had been repaid. She explains she has used it to buy fine clothes. *The Shipman's Tale*

37

Marcian, Marcien: Martianus Mineus Felix Capella, of Carthage in the 5th century, author of *De Nuptiis Philologiae et Mercurii*. *The Merchant's Tale*

Marcus Tullius Cicero: Cicero (106–43 B.C.), a Roman Republican orator and philosopher. His chief works include *De Oratore, De Republica, De Senectute, De Natura Deorum*. *The Franklin's Prologue*

Mark: It is not St. Mark but St. John who speaks of the five *barley* loaves and two small fishes that feed the five thousand. The Wife of Bath makes the reference, equating wives with 'barly-breed' and saints with bread made from pure wheat. *The Wife of Bath's Prologue*

MARS: The god of war, identified with the Greek god Ares, and regarded as the son of Juno (Hera). Theseus builds a stadium and three temples, of Venus, Diana and Mars, for the tournament. 'The nexte houre of Mars folwinge this, Arcite un-to the temple walked is Of fierce Mars to doon his sacrifyse.' Arcite prays to Mars and is victorious in the tournament, but Palamon prays to Venus, and wins the lady Emily. *The Knight's Tale*

Mathew: According to St. Matthew, 'The heighe god forbad swering at al', which the Pardoner thoroughly supports. *The Pardoner's Tale*

MAUNCIPLE: The Manciple is employed at an Inn of Court. His duties include the purchasing of provisions, keeping of accounts and supervising the cook. He uses his position to cheat the group of students and learned men, his masters (a dozen of them fit to be stewards to the peerage), by means of shrewdness and practical experience in careful marketing. He certainly does well for himself. *The Prologue*

Maure, Seint: St. Maur (Maurus) d. A.D. 565, a disciple of St. Benedict. The rules of these two men established monasticism in Europe, but are not much regarded by the Monk. *The Prologue*

MAURICE: The son of Constance and Alla, King of Northumberland. After early unhappiness he becomes Emperor in Rome. *The Man of Law's Tale*

Maximus: A Roman officer under Almachius. He was converted to Christianity by the preaching of the brothers Valerian and Tiburtius, who were his prisoners. Maximus himself converted many, and for this was scourged to death with whips of lead. *The Second Nun's Tale*

MEDEA: A magician, daughter of Aeëtes, King of Colchis. She and Jason fell in love when he came to Colchis in quest of the golden fleece. Her enchantments included restoring Jason's father Aeson to youth by boiling him in a cauldron with magic herbs. She had a gruesome way of destroying her enemies. *The Knight's Tale; Introduction* to *The Man of Law's Tale*

MELEAGRE: Meleager, son of Oeneus, lord of Calydon, and Althaea. He slew the Calydonian boar, and gave the head to Atalanta, who had been first to wound it. *The Knight's Tale*

MELIBEUS: Melibee and his wife Prudence have a long debate on whether a violent injury should be avenged by violence. The subject arises because in Melibee's absence three old enemies have broken in, beaten Prudence and left their daughter Sophia with five wounds from which she may or may not recover. The men are found and Melibee first decides to let them off with a fine, but Prudence persuades him to forgive them completely. *Tale of Melibee*

MERCURYE: Mercury, called Hermes by the Romans, and

said to be the son of Zeus and Maia. Inventor of the lyre and messenger of the gods, he wore winged sandals, a broad-brimmed hat and carried a sleep-producing wand, 'caduceus'. The god appears to Arcite one night, and orders him to go to Athens. *The Knight's Tale*

MIDA: Midas, the semi-legendary, wealthy King of Phrygia. He declared Pan to be a better flute-player than Apollo, who, angered, turned his ears into those of an ass. Ovid tells the story of the wife of Midas, who, unable to keep the secret, whispers it to the waters of a marsh. *The Wife of Bath's Tale*

MILLERE: A quarrelsome lout, the first to oppose the Host in his capacity as master of ceremonies. 'He was short-sholdred, brood, a thikke knarre', with a red spade-shaped beard, a wart on his nose, flaring nostrils and a large mouth. He excels at wrestling, has crude, primitive vigour, and tells coarse tales. He steals flour, and increases his fee by milling three times over. He is talkative, quickly angered, and a liar. As the pilgrims leave Southwark, he plays the bagpipes. *The Prologue*

Moises: Moses is mentioned when people speak of Canace's magic ring for he 'hadde a name of konning in swich art'. *The Squire's Tale;* also mentioned in *The Summoner's Tale*

MONK: This hunting cleric, owner of horses and greyhounds, is an 'outridere', or supervisor of the outlying dependent houses of a large monastery. He is fond of hunting, fine clothes and splendid food. Plump and worldly, he has turned away from godliness to gross self-indulgence. This 'manly man' defends his untraditional conduct, and 'yaf nat of that text a pulled hen, That seith that hunters been nat holy men'. *The Prologue*

N

Nabal: The husband of Abigail, who saved him from being slain (1 Samuel 25). *The Merchant's Tale*

Nabugodonosor: Nebuchadnezzar, the King of Babylonia 605–562 B.C., who from the glories of wealth and power went mad, 'and lyk a beste him semed for to be, And eet hay as an oxe'. When he was restored to sanity, he repented of his sins and swore to sin no more, according to the Monk. *The Monk's Tale*

NARCISUS: Narcissus, beautiful son of the river-god Cephissus and the nymph Liriope. Entranced by his image reflected in water, he is driven to despair and death. *The Knight's Tale*

Nero: A Roman emperor from A.D. 54 to 68, his viciousness and tyranny became proverbial. He killed his brother, mutilated his mother, and killed Seneca in a bath. He burnt Rome. His subjects revolted against his oppression. In a garden, before two peasants, he killed himself as the soldiers sent to destroy him appeared. *The Monk's Tale; The Knight's Tale*

Nessus: Centaur killed by Hercules. *The Monk's Tale*

Newe Rachel: This name was given to the mother of the chorister murdered by the Jews. Rachel was the mother of one of the infants murdered by Herod. *The Prioress's Tale*

NICERATES WYF: Niceratus was put to death by the Thirty Tyrants; his wife took her own life. *The Franklin's Tale*

Nichanore: Nicanor, a general defeated and slain by Judas Maccabeus. *The Monk's Tale*

NICHOLAS: The clerk who lodges with John, the old carpenter at Oxford. He loves Alison, John's young wife, and persuades John to hang three tubs in the roof in expectation of a flood. With John in his tub, Nicholas makes love to Alison. Absalon, also in love with her, kisses what Alison presents to him at the window—her bare bottom. In anger he fetches a hot iron. This time Nicholas sits on the window-sill for a joke, and his bottom is scorched. *The Miller's Tale*

Nicholas: St. Nicholas who, according to legend, even as a baby refused to eat on fast-days. *The Prioress's Tale*

NONNE: The Nun is chaplain (secretary and assistant) to the Prioress. *The Prologue*

NONNES PREEST: The Nun's Priest is announced to every-one by the Host as 'This swete preest, this goodly man, sir John'. Always modest, he is highly intelligent with a pleasant sense of humour. *The Prologue; The Nun's Priest's Prologue*

One of the three priests in attendance on the First Nun, the Prioress. *The Prologue*

NORICE, NORYS: A nurse. Chanticleer tells Pertelote of how St. Kenelm, when seven years old, saw his murder in a dream; his nurse explained the dream, warning him of treason. *The Nun's Priest's Tale*

Nowelis: Nowelis flood is a humorous blunder on the part of the Miller for 'Noes', Noah's. *The Miller's Tale*

O

Odenake: Odenathus, ruler of Palmyra, husband of Cenobia. *The Monk's Tale*

OLD MAN: The three rioters, setting out to find and kill Death, meet 'an oold man and a poore', who also seeks Death, but not in order to defeat him. Simple and elemental, he understands Death, is mysteriously 'al forwrapped', and may be more than he appears to be. His information leads the three rioters to their death. *The Pardoner's Tale*

OLIFAUNT, SIR: Sir Elephant, a three-headed giant, fiercely orders Sir Thopas away when he encroaches on the territory of 'the queen of Fayerye'. Sir Thopas withdraws to arm himself for a fight the next day. *The Tale of Sir Thopas*

Oloferne, Oloferno, Olofernus: Holofernes, Nebuchadnezzar's ruthless general, was killed by Judith in his tent before the walls of Bethulia (Jerusalem). *The Monk's Tale; The Tale of Melibee*

Olyver: Oliver, one of the twelve chivalrous knights of Charlemagne; a friend of Roland. *The Monk's Tale*

Omer: Homer, the great Greek epic poet, probably of the 9th century B.C., author of the *Iliad* and the *Odyssey*. In the latter, he tells of Penelope, who was faithful to her husband, Odysseus, during his absence of twenty years. *The Franklin's Tale*

OSEWOLD: Oswald, *see* Reve

Ovide: Ovid, the Roman poet (43 B.C.–A.D. 18), whose chief works were the *Amores, Ars Amatoria, Metamorphoses,* and *Fasti*. He was the favourite Latin poet of the Middle Ages. *The Wife of Bath's Tale; Introduction* to *The Man of Law's Tale*

43

P

PALAMON: Arcite's cousin. The two young nobles are both imprisoned by Theseus after the fall of Thebes. They see Emily in the garden and fall in love with her. Arcite is released and leaves Athens. Palamon escapes some years later. He meets a changed Arcite in a field relating his life story. They fight a duel, now in anger, the winner to woo Emily. Theseus stops the duel and arranges a grand tournament, in which Palamon is captured by Arcite and his knights. Arcite is declared the winner, but his horse throws him and he dies. Theseus declares that Athens should have peace, and that Palamon and Emily should be married. *The Knight's Tale*

PALLAS: Athene, the Greek goddess of wisdom. In praising Virginia, the heroine of his story, the Physician says 'she were wys as Pallas, dar I seyn'. *The Physician's Tale*

PAMPHILLES: Pamphilus, hero of the Latin dialogue *Pamphilus de Amore*. *The Tale of Melibee*

PARDONER: Probably in minor orders, and attached to the hospital of the Blessed ¦Mary of Rouncivalle,¦ near Charing Cross, the Pardoner has just returned from Rome. Without requiring penitence, he sells papal indulgences as instant pardons. He is effeminate in appearance, with hair 'as yelow as wex' hanging like a hank of flax, glaring eyes, a voice 'smal as hath a goot', and he will never grow a beard. A consummate hypocrite, he enjoys exploiting human credulity and ignorant superstition. His bag is stuffed with false religious relics—bones of saints which are really 'pigges bones', and 'Oure Lady veyl' (a pillowcase). By selling these, he takes in one day more than an honest parson earns in a month. In church, he acts a part, singing the

44

offertory well in order 'to wynne silver'. In the Prologue to his *Tale* he freely confesses his confidence tricks and his avarice. At the end of his tale he turns to the Host and claims he is 'moost envoluped in synne' and therefore should kiss all his relics—for a groat. The Host reviles him in the strongest language. *The Prologue*

Paul: St. Paul, asserts the Pardoner, declared that those who give way to gluttony and make a god of their stomachs are enemies of Christ's cross and will suffer death for it. *The Pardoner's Tale*

PENELOPEE, PENELOPE: The faithful wife of Ulysses (Odysseus). *Introduction* to *The Man of Law's Tale; The Franklin's Tale*

PENNEUS DOGHTER: Daphne, daughter of Peneus, a river-god, was pursued by Apollo, but called upon her mother and was changed into a laurel. *The Knight's Tale*

PERCYVELL: The hero of the romance *Sir Percyvelle of Galles. The Tale of Sir Thopas*

PERKYN REVELOUR: Perkin is an apprentice in the victual-ling trade, who neglects the Cheapside shop where he works for dancing, drinking, dice and easy girls. He is sacked, and joins another young man, whose wife 'swyved for hir sustenance'. *The Cook's Tale*

PEROTHEUS: Pirithous, friend of Theseus and of Arcite. He obtains Arcite's release from prison. *The Knight's Tale*

PERSOUN: The Parson is a learned man, poor, 'but riche . . . of holy thoght and werk'. He is a good man, 'a shep-herde and no mercenarie'. He is loath to excommunicate anyone for not paying tithes, and helps the poor with money from the general collection or from his own limited 'substaunce'. His life is one of perfect Christian charity. He teaches the gospel, and follows its doctrines himself. *The Prologue*

Petrak, Petrark: Petrarch; Francesco Petrarca (1304–74), was an Italian poet and humanist who lived mostly in Provence, and was crowned poet laureate at Rome in 1341. He is famous for his love-poetry inspired by Laura. He translated the story of Griselda into Latin from the *Decameron*, by his friend Boccaccio. This work was possibly Chaucer's source for *The Clerk's Tale*. *The Clerk's Tale*

Petro Rege de Cipro: Pierre de Lusignan became King of Cyprus in 1352 and was assassinated in 1369. Like Peter of Spain he was known to the English court; in 1363 he was entertained by Edward III. Chaucer's Knight appears to have seen service with him. *The Monk's Tale*

Petro Rege Ispannie: Pedro, King of Castile and Leon (1350–69) was killed by his brother, Don Enrique, who, the Monk says, was not a friend, but a traitor like Ganelon. Professor Robinson suggests that Chaucer had several reasons for interest in Pedro of Spain: the Black Prince fought with him against Enrique in 1367; then in 1371 John of Gaunt married Pedro's daughter Constance, and assumed in her right the title of King of Castile and Leon; also, Chaucer's wife Philippa appears to have been attached to her household for a couple of years after her arrival in England. *The Monk's Tale*

Phanye: Phanýa was the daughter of Croesus, last King of Lydia, 560–546 B.C. *The Monk's Tale*

Pharao: Pharaoh, the name of the kings of Egypt. Chanticleer, speaking to Pertelote, refers to 'daun Pharao, his bakere and his boteler also' in his examples of those who had dreamed meaningful dreams. *The Nun's Priest's Tale*

PHASIPHA: Pasiphaë, the wife of Minos, King of Crete. She loves a white bull and becomes the mother of the Minotaur, part man, part bull, which Minos keeps in a labyrinth at Knossos. *The Wife of Bath's Prologue*

PHEBUS: He is a great warrior, loves his wife, but is extremely jealous. He has a white-feathered crow that can counterfeit any man's speech, and thus reveals his wife's infidelity. In anger Phoebus kills his wife. Filled with remorse, he plucks out all the white feathers and 'make him blak, and refte him al his song', then throws the crow to the Devil. *The Manciple's Tale*

Phidoun: Phidon was slain by the Thirty Tyrants (the cruel government imposed on the Athenians after the capture of Athens by Lysander in 404 B.C.). His daughters were captured and brought naked to the tyrants' feast, but 'rather than they wolde lese hir maydenhede' they escaped their guard and drowned themselves in a well. *The Franklin's Tale*

PHILLIS: Phyllis, the beloved of Demophon. *Introduction* to *The Man of Law's Tale*

PHILOSTRATE: Philostratus, meaning 'vanquished by love', is the name assumed by Arcite when for a year or two he remains with Emily as her 'page of the chambre'. *The Knight's Tale*

Phitonesse, Phitonissa: Pythoness, the name often applied to the Witch of Endor, the woman with 'a familiar spirit' consulted by Saul when God had forsaken him and the Philistines threatened. She called up Samuel. It was believed that the Devil came in his stead to prove that the Devil could pass as a good man. *The Friar's Tale*

PHITOUN: The Python personifies the dark forces of the underworld and is guardian of Delphi. Phoebus destroys the Python and seizes Delphi. *The Manciple's Tale*

47

PIERIDES: The Muses, from Pieria on the slopes of Mount Olympus. Chaucer refers to Ovid's *Metamorphoses*, in which the daughters of King Pierus of Emathia compete with the Muses and are turned into magpies. *Introduction* to *The Man of Law's Tale*

Piers Alfonce: Petrus Alphonsus, Spanish author of the *Disciplina Clericalis*. *The Tale of Melibee*

PIGMALION: Pygmalion, a King of Cyprus and a sculptor. He made a beautiful statue of a woman, and at his prayer Aphrodite brought it to life. *The Physician's Tale*

Pilate: Pilate's voice. Pilate (and Herod) were represented as boisterous characters in the miracle-plays. *The Miller's Prologue*

PIRAMUS: Pyramus, a youth of Babylon, in love with Thisbe. *The Merchant's Tale*

PIRRUS: Pyrrhus, the son of Achilles, revenged his father's death by killing King Priam. The noise of the lamentations of the Trojan noblewomen when Troy fell and Priam was killed is surpassed by that made by all the hens in the enclosure in this tale. *The Nun's Priest's Tale*

PLACEBO: A friend of January's who advises him on his marriage to May. *The Merchant's Tale*

Plato: The words of this Greek philosopher (*c.* 427–348 B.C.) are quoted by the Manciple: 'The word moot nede accorde with the dede.' *The Manciple's Tale*

PLEYNDAMOUR: A typical hero of a romance. *The Tale of Sir Thopas*

48

PLOWMAN: The Ploughman, the Parson's brother, is a true worker, simple and virtuous in his actions, who helps the poor without payment. He loves first God and then his neighbour as himself, and lives 'in pees and parfit charitee'. *The Prologue*

PLUTO: God of the underworld, son of Cronos and Thea, and brother of Zeus and Poseidon. In the Temple of Diana, the goddess is depicted in wall-paintings contemplating Pluto's domain ('Hir eyen caste she ful lowe adoun, Ther Pluto hath his derke regioun'). He sends down, at the request of Saturn, an 'infernal fury' which causes Arcite to fall from his horse after his triumph in the tournament. *The Knight's Tale*

Being ruler of the underworld where medieval folk thought fairies lived, he is represented here as King of the Fairies. He restores January's sight on condition that Proserpina will provide May's excuse to her husband for apparently making love with Damian in a pear-tree. *The Merchant's Tale*

Pompeius: Pompey 'The Great' (106–48 B.C.), a famous Roman general who opposed Julius Caesar and was defeated at Pharsalus. *The Monk's Tale*

Porcia: Portia, the virtuous wife of Marcus Brutus. *The Franklin's Tale*

PRIAM: The last King of Troy, killed at the taking of the city by Pyrrhus, son of Achilles. *The Nun's Priest's Tale*

PRIAPUS: The god of fertility, son of Dionysus and Aphrodite. The Merchant describes January's house, finery and handsome garden, which are beyond the eloquence of Priapus himself. *The Merchant's Tale*

PRIORESSE: Madam Eglentyne (meaning 'sweet-briar'), the Prioress, is probably the head of a convent of some importance. She is a handsome woman with exquisite manners, elegance in dress, a stately bearing, and speaks French—not Parisian French, but that of Stratford-atte-Bowe, the Benedictine nunnery of St. Leonard's at Bromley. Charming though she is, the sympathies of her tender heart probably go no further than her concern for trapped mice and the diet of her pampered small dogs. *The Prologue*

PROSERPYNA, PROSERPYNE: Proserpina, wife of Pluto, who provides May's excuse when she is seen by January (his sight restored by Pluto) making love with Damian in a pear-tree. May tells her husband that his sight is still imperfect and she was only struggling with a man in the tree. January gladly accepts this. *The Merchant's Tale*

PROTHESELAUS: Protesilaus, a Thessalian prince, husband of Laodamia, was killed by the Trojans as he landed in their country. *The Franklin's Tale*

PROVOST: This man condemns the Jews of an Asian ghetto who have murdered a seven-year-old chorister ('clergeoun') to be drawn apart by wild horses, then hanged from a cart. *The Prioress's Tale*

PRUDENCE: The merciful Dame Prudence has a long disputation with Melibee, her husband, on how to deal with enemies who have grievously harmed them. She has been beaten and their daughter Sophie wounded five times by three intruders. When these men are caught, Prudence persuades Melibee to forgive them. *The Tale of Milibee*

Ptholome, Tholome: Ptolemy, Claudius Ptolemaeus, a celebrated astronomer of the 2nd century A.D. In his *Mathematike Syntaxis*, translated later into Arabic and known as the *Almagest*, he summed up the known astronomy of the age. He developed a theory that the planets move round the stationary earth. The Wife of Bath quotes this proverb from the *Almagest*: 'Of alle men his wisdom is the hyeste, That rekketh never who hath the world in honde.' *The Wife of Bath's Prologue*

R

Razis: Rhazes, a Spanish Arab physician of the 10th century A.D., with whose works the Doctor (or Physician) is familiar. *The Prologue*

Rebekka, Rebekke: Rebecca, whose son Jacob took her good advice and won 'his fadres benisoun', is praised by January. *The Merchant's Tale*

REVE: Oswald, the Reeve, comes from Baldeswell in Norfolk. He is the manager of a manorial estate, supervising work and keeping accounts. Admired by his employers, whom he cheats, he is feared by the workers in his charge 'as of the deeth'. He is thin, bad-tempered, efficient and cunning; no auditor 'koude on him wynne'. He has a 'fair house upon a heath', perhaps attained because 'his lord wel koude he plesen subtilly', by giving and loaning to him his own goods. Oswald is also a skilled carpenter. He rides last of all the pilgrims. *The Prologue*

Richard: Richard I, who was wounded by an arrow on Friday, 26 March 1199, when besieging Vidomar, Viscount of Limoges, in the castle of Chalus. Richard died shortly after, on 6 April. *The Nun's Priest's Tale*

ROBYN: Robin, the serving-lad who helps John the carpenter, his master, to heave the door of Nicholas's room off its hinges. *The Miller's Tale*

Rodogone: Rhodogone, the virtuous daughter of Darius the Great (King of Persia, 521–485 B.C.). *The Franklin's Tale*

ROGER: *see* Cook

Rufus: A Greek physician of Ephesus in the time of Trajan (A.D. 98–117). He wrote works on anatomy. *The Prologue*

RYOTOURES THREE: After denouncing the sins of lechery, gluttony, drunkenness, gambling, swearing, perjury and homicide, the Pardoner tells a tale of three rioters who, in times of plague, leave a tavern to search for Death, who has just killed one of their comrades. They speak roughly to an old man, who tells them they will find Death under a certain tree. There they discover a heap of golden florins. The youngest is sent to fetch bread and wine, and poisons two of the three bottles. On his return the other two kill him with their daggers, then each drinks from a poisoned bottle and they both die. *The Pardoner's Tale*

S

Salamon, Salomon: Solomon, son of David and Bathsheba, King of Israel, 10th century B.C. He became a symbol of wisdom and magnificence, but was also dissipated, and had many wives. In the wall-paintings of the Temple of Venus is depicted the 'folye of King Salamon'. *The Knight's Tale; The Cook's Prologue*

Solomon, mentioned when Canace's magic ring is acclaimed, was thought to have supernatural powers. *The Squire's Tale*

Sampsoun: Samson, warrior of Zion, told his love, Delilah, that his power lay within his hair. She bade his enemies clip his hair, then they put out his eyes and held him prisoner. Later at a feast he caused two pillars to fall and a whole temple to be destroyed, killing himself and 'eek his fo-men alle'. *The Monk's Tale*

Samuel: A Hebrew prophet who made Saul king of Israel. Saul, when forsaken by God and in fear of the Philistines, consulted the Witch of Endor. To please him she called up Samuel, who spoke of the death of Saul and the defeat of his army. *The Friar's Tale*

Sapor: Shapur I, King of Persia, 3rd century A.D. *The Monk's Tale*

SATHANAS: Satan. *The Friar's Tale; The Summoner's Tale*

SATURNE: Saturn, identified with the Greek Cronos, a god of agriculture. The anger of Saturn against Thebes is recalled by Palamon in prison ('Saturne, And eek . . . Juno, jalous and eek wood, . . . hath destroyed wel ny al the blood Of Thebes'). *The Knight's Tale*

Scariot: Judas Iscariot the traitor. *The Nun's Priest's Tale*

Scipioun: Scipio Africanus Minor (*c.* 185–129 B.C.), a fine orator and distinguished soldier, who destroyed Carthage in 146. *Somnium Scipionis*, 'The Dream of Scipio', is part of Cicero's *De Republica* telling in a dream the future of Scipio's life. *The Nun's Priest's Tale*

Senek: Seneca, the Roman author, made a comparison between madness and drunkenness, according to the Pardoner. *The Pardoner's Tale; Introduction* to *The Man of Law's Tale*

Serapion: This name was borne by three medical writers.

Perhaps the last of these, an Arabian of the 11th or 12th century who wrote *Liber de Medicamentis Simplicibus*, is the one whose works the Doctor of Physic knows. *The Prologue*

SERGEANT OF THE LAWE: An able lawyer, the Man of Law receives large fees and talks as though he knows all the cases and judgments in law since the time of William the Conqueror. His 'purchasyng' may be done largely on his own account. He appears to be the busiest of men, 'and yet he semed bisier than he was'. In the introduction to his tale he tells us that Chaucer has written more of lovers than Ovid (among them Lucrece, Thisbe, Aeneas, Phyllis, Demophon, Dejanira and Hermione, Ariadne, Hypsipyle, Leander, Hero, Briseis, Helen, Laodamia, Hypermnestra and Penelope). *The Prologue*

SHIPMAN: Probably from Dartmouth, he is a good navigator, proficient in seamanship, skipper of *The Maudelayne*, and knows all ports from the Baltic to Spain. He travels armed for defence or attack. If he overcomes an enemy vessel, he drowns the prisoners. He often steals wine from Bordeaux, while the chapman sleeps: 'Of nyce conscience took he no keep.' *The Prologue*

SIMON, SYMOND: Alan and John, the two bible clerks, call the miller by this name in the story. *The Reeve's Tale*

Socrates: The Greek philosopher (469–399 B.C.), whose splendid teaching is preserved in the *Dialogues* of Plato his pupil. *The Wife of Bath's Prologue*

SOMNOUR: The Summoner bears summons to an ecclesiastical court of law, sees that offenders appear in court, and looks sharply for indictable offences. By threatening sinners who fear excommunication he can easily obtain bribes to keep him silent, and he uses blackmail when necessary. His fire-red, carbuncular face, narrow eyes and black scabby eyebrows frighten children. When drunk he repeats a few Latin tags such as *'Questio quid juris?'* to impress people. This loathsome, corrupt man is given to gluttony, drunkenness, and lechery. *The Prologue*

Working for an archdeacon is a false, vulgar, conceited summoner. He meets a yeoman who claims to be a bailiff then admits he is really a fiend from hell. They reach a widow's house. The summoner tries to get twelve pence from her, but as she has not that sum he demands her new pan in payment. She consigns him and the pan to the Devil. The yeoman finds it is her true desire; the summoner will not repent, and so, as a fiend, he carries him off to hell. *The Friar's Tale*

SOPHIE: Daughter of Melibee and Prudence. Three intruders wound her five times and severely beat her mother. This leads her parents to debate on whether to avenge violent injury with violence. In the end they forgive the miscreants. *The Tale of Melibee*

SOWDAN OF SURRYE: Sultan of Syria who becomes a Christian to marry Constance, daughter of the Emperor of Rome. He is murdered with his fellow converts by his mother and her supporters at the marriage feast in Syria. *The Man of Law's Tale*

SQUIER: The Squire, son of the Knight, is a typical courtly lover, twenty years of age, agile and strong. He has fought in Flanders, Artois and Picardy in hope of winning his lady's favour, but is also serving his probation for the honours of knighthood. He dresses well, and is singing, fluting, and dancing all day, 'as fressh as is the month of May'. He is courteous and humble, and carves for his father at the table. *The Prologue*

Stace: Statius (*c.* A.D. 40–96), Roman poet, author of a

Thebaid on the expedition of the Seven against Thebes. The rites performed by Emily in the Temple of Diana on the morning of the tournament are described in this work. *The Knight's Tale*

STILBOUN: The Pardoner relates how this high-principled ambassador goes to Corinth and finds the very nobles playing dice. He refuses to make an alliance between Sparta, his country, and such a place. *The Pardoner's Tale*

Straw, Jakke: Jack Straw, the leader of a party of rebels from Essex in the Peasants' Revolt of 1381. They killed a number of Flemings in the Vintry, but the noise of the massacre was not as great as the hue and cry after the fox in this tale. *The Nun's Priest's Tale*

Stymphalides: Stymphalis, a woman loved by Aristoclides, a Greek tyrant. *The Franklin's Tale*

SYMKYN: Simkin or Simpkin (diminutive of Simon), the miller at Trumpington near Cambridge. He is a bully and also steals corn from his customers. When John and Alan, students from Solar Hall, bring corn for grinding, Simpkin lets their horse loose on the fen. By the time they return with it night has fallen and he has stolen half their flour. Obliged to stay the night, the two students join the family, husband, wife, daughter and baby, in their one bedroom. With ingenuity and luck Alan sleeps with the daughter, John with the wife. Alan, by mistake, later joins the miller. This leads to a fight in which the wife in error strikes down her husband and the bible-clerks escape. *The Reeve's Tale*

SYNOUN: The Greek Sinon who allowed himself to be captured by the Trojans. He then persuaded them to drag into Troy the wooden horse in which Greek soldiers were concealed. The fox, like Sinon, is a false deceiver. *The Nun's Priest's Tale; The Squire's Tale*

T

TESBEE, TISBE: Thisbe, a girl of Babylon, in love with Pyramus. Like May and Damian, these lovers had to resort to trickery. *The Merchant's Tale; Introduction* to *The Man of Law's Tale*

Teuta: A chaste wife, Queen of Illyria in 231 B.C. *The Franklin's Tale*

THELOPHUS: Telephus, son-in-law of Priam, King of Troy. He was wounded by the spear of Achilles, then healed by dust from the spear. *The Squire's Tale*

THEODOMAS: Thiodamas, a Theban soothsayer. *The Merchant's Tale*

THEODORA: The Squire is about to tell us how Algarsyf wins Theodora to wife, when the Franklin interrupts and the story is left unfinished. *The Squire's Tale*

Theofraste: Theophrastus, a Greek philosopher, flourished in the 3rd century B.C. He wrote *Liber Aureolus de Nuptiis*, a book disparaging marriage, which the elderly knight, January, condemns as false, for he now wishes to be married. *The Merchant's Tale*

THESEUS: Duke of Athens and a distinguished soldier; he conquers Scythia, ruled by the Amazons, and returns home with his wife Hippolyta and her sister Emily. Confronted by some grief-stricken women who have lost their husbands during the siege of Thebes, he goes there immediately, defeats the tyrant King Creon, sacks Thebes, and imprisons for life two young Theban cousins, Palamon and Arcite. On the request of his friend Perotheus he releases Arcite. Palamon escapes some years later. These two meet

57

and fight a duel, the winner to woo Emily. Theseus stops the duel and arranges instead a grand tournament. He builds a magnificent stadium and temples to Venus, Mars and Diana, with splendid wall-paintings. When Arcite dies he makes preparations for a ceremonial funeral, and arranges the marriage of Palamon and Emily, a union between Athens and Thebes. *The Knight's Tale*

THOMAS: From his sick-bed this man defeats the manœuvres of a greedy, bombastic, hypocritical friar in his demands for gold. Instead he offers an unsavoury gift to be divided among friars equally: 'Ther nis no capul, drawinge in a cart, That mighte have lete a fart of swich a soun.' Later Jankin suggests how this equal division should be made. *The Summoner's Tale*

Thomas, Seint; Thomas of Kent, Seint: St. Thomas à Becket, assassinated in 1170, whose shrine at Canterbury (the pilgrims' destination) was famous in England and in Europe. The sick, especially, sought his intercession. *The Prologue; The Miller's Tale*

Thomas of Ynde: St. Thomas, whose missionary work in India is mentioned by St. Jerome. *The Merchant's Prologue*

THOPAS, SIR: A Knight-errant who dreams of an elf-queen and sets out to find her. He encounters Sir Elephant, a giant. After fierce words, Sir Thopas withdraws to arm for a fight the next day. *The Tale of Sir Thopas*

THYMOTHEE: Timotheus, a Jew, vanquished by the Seleucids. *The Monk's Tale*

Tiburce: Tiburtius, Valerian's brother, who under the influence of the angel and the two coronals of roses and lilies and the words of Cecilia was converted. Later he was beheaded. *The Second Nun's Tale*

Titus Livius: Livy (59 B.C.–A.D. 17), the Roman historian, friend of Emperor Augustus. He wrote the history of Rome from its foundation to the death of Drusus in 9 B.C. *The Physician's Tale*

Trotula: Probably a renowned woman doctor of Salermo of the 11th century, named by the Wife of Bath when referring to the reading-matter of John, her fifth husband. *The Wife of Bath's Prologue*

Tullius: *see* Marcus Tullius Cicero

TULLIUS HOSTILIUS: Tullus Hostilius, one of the legendary kings of Rome, who rose to power, fought with Alba, and extended Rome. *The Wife of Bath's Tale*

TURNUS: King of the Rutuli, betrothed to Lavinia. A spirited man and fiery warrior, he was killed by Aeneas. He appears in the wall-drawings in the temple of Venus in this tale. *The Knight's Tale;* also mentioned in *The Man of Law's Tale*

U

Urban: Pope Urban I, beheaded A.D. 230, then became a martyr, St. Urban. Valerian goes to see him, and later his wife, Cecilia, is buried with Urban's saints. *The Second Nun's Tale*

V

VALERIA: The virtuous wife of Servius. *The Franklin's Tale*

VALERIAN: The husband of Cecilia and brother of Tiburtius, he was converted by her to Christianity; all suffered martyrdom in Rome. *The Second Nun's Tale*

VALERIUS: Valerius Maximus, the Latin author of *Facta et Dicta Memorabilia. The Monk's Tale; The Wife of Bath's Tale*

VENUS: Identified with the Aphrodite of the Greeks as the goddess of love and beauty. She rose from the foam of the sea near the island of Cythera and was often called Cytherea. Theseus builds an altar and an oratory to her where Palamon invokes the goddess's aid. *The Knight's Tale*

VIRGILE, VIRGILIUS: Virgil, the Latin poet (70–19 B.C.). His chief works were the *Aeneid*, the *Georgics*, and the *Eclogues* or *Bucolics. The Friar's Tale*

VIRGINIA: The beautiful, virtuous daughter of a knight, Virginius. A judge, Appius, desires her, and tells a servant, Claudius, to claim she was stolen as a child and must be returned. In court Appius says she should be his ward first of all. Virginius tells her she must choose death or shame. She chooses death. He cuts off her head, and sends it to the judge in court. *The Physician's Tale*

VIRGINIUS: A knight, father of Virginia. A wicked judge, Appius, accepts the false story from Claudius that she was stolen as a child. Desiring to seduce her, he rules that she should be his ward before her return. Virginia chooses death rather than shame, so her father cuts off her head and sends it to the judge. *The Physician's Tale*

Vitulon: Witelo, a Polish physicist of the 13th century. *The Squire's Tale*

VULCANUS: Palamon kneels to pray near the Temple of Venus to 'Faireste of fair, O lady myn, Venus, Doghter to Jove and spouse of Vulcanus'. Venus is the wife of Vulcan in the *Odyssey*, where they are identified with the Greek Aphrodite and Hephaestus. *The Knight's Tale*

W

WADE: A hero of Anglo-Saxon antiquity of whom little is known. His boat was called *Guingelot*. *The Merchant's Tale*

WALTER: The Marquis of Saluzzo in Italy who marries the humble Griselda. They have a daughter and a son. Selfish and cruel, the Marquis tries Griselda's goodness and patience severely. For a time he sends her back to her father. Walter says he has proved her submissiveness; she returns and from that time 'liven thise two in concord and in reste'. *The Clerk's Tale*

WARDEYN: The Warden of Solar Hall, Cambridge, who, angered at the miller's thefts, allows two students, John and Alan, to visit him. *The Reeve's Tale*

WIDWE: The poor widow of temperate habits with two daughters dwells in a small cottage, caring for a cock, seven hens, three sows, three cows and a sheep. All join in a frenzied chase at the end, when Chanticleer escapes from the fox. *The Nun's Priest's Tale*

WIF OF BISIDE BATHE: Dame Alice, the Wife of Bath, is the most experienced pilgrim of them all. She has been three times to the Holy Land, and on pilgrimages to Rome, Boulogne-sur-mer, Galicia (the shrine of St James of Compostella), and Cologne (the shrine of the Three Kings). 'She koude muchel of wandrynge by the weye.' She is a skilful cloth-maker, a woman of property with no problems over dowries, and has been married five times. Happy marriages to her are those where the wife is firmly in control. She is a new social figure, boisterous, opulent, adventurous and dominating. Venus, she says, gives her amorous desire, and Mars a sturdy hardiness. She shows these and other qualities in her vivid monologue. 'In felaweshipe wel koude she laughe and carpe. Of remedies of love she knew per chaunce, For she koude of that art the olde daunce.' *The Prologue*

WILKYN: Wilkin, a name given by the Wife of Bath to one of her husbands: 'gode lief, tak keep How mekely loketh Wilkyn, oure sheep! Com neer, my spouse, lat me ba thy cheke!' *The Wife of Bath's Prologue*

WYF: The wife of Phoebus. Her infidelity is revealed to her husband by the white crow's descriptive speech. Phoebus kills her in anger. *The Manciple's Tale*

WYF OF MARCHANT: The wife of the mean merchant. *The Shipman's Tale*

X

Xantippa: Xantippe, the wife of Socrates, believed to have been a scold. *The Wife of Bath's Prologue*

Y

YEMAN: The Yeoman is a kind of bailiff or gamekeeper on the Knight's estate. 'A not-heed hadde he, with a broun visage.' He is disciplined and efficient, with sword, dagger, and buckler in fighting trim, 'and in his hand he bar a mighty bowe', the famous national weapon. A lively, vigorous figure he 'was clad in cote and hood of green', the woodman's colour. *The Prologue*

This yeoman claims to be a bailiff but later admits he is really a fiend from hell. He strikes up a friendship with a summoner, who tries to extort money, then a pan, from a poor widow, who commends him to the Devil. The fiend then takes him off to hell. *The Friar's Tale*

YPERMYSTRA: Hypermnestra, daughter of Danaus. *Introduction* to *The Man of Law's Tale*

Ypocras: Hippocrates, a great Greek physician, born on the Aegean island of Cos about 460 B.C. The founder of Greek medical science, he was regarded by his contemporaries as the perfect type of physician, 'learned, humane, grave and reticent'. *The Prologue*

YPOLITA: Hippolyta, leader of the Amazons and wife of Theseus. He is determined to defeat Creon, and sends his wife and Emily 'hir yonge suster shene, Un-to the toun of Athenes to dwelle' before he marches to Thebes with his army. *The Knight's Tale*

YPOTYS: Hypotis, hero of medieval romance. *The Tale of Sir Thopas*

Z

Zanzis, Zeuxis: A famous painter of Greece in the 5th century B.C. Chaucer wrongly thought he was a writer. *The Physician's Tale*

Animals in Part One

BAYARD: A horse owned by the Warden of Solar Hall, Cambridge. He lends it to John and Alan, bible-students, to take corn to the miller to be ground. The miller lets the horse loose on the fen and the students do not recover it till nightfall. *The Reeve's Tale*

BROK: Brock, one of the horses pulling a farm-cart loaded with hay to a standstill in a muddy lane. The carter shouts on the Devil to take them all. The summoner standing near with the fiend tells him to accept the offer. The fiend replies that the carter did not mean what he said. *The Friar's Tale*

BURNEL THE ASSE: The fox tells Chanticleer that he has read a story in *Burnel the Ass* of a young man, Gundulfus, who broke a cock's leg by throwing a stone at it. Later a bishop was to ordain Gundulfus, but the cock in revenge crowed so late that Gundulfus overslept and lost his benefice. *The Nun's Priest's Tale*

CERBERUS: The dog with either two, three or many heads who guarded the entrance to Hades. In one of his Twelve Labours, Hercules drove out 'the hound of helle'. *The Monk's Tale*

CHAUNTECLEER: Chanticleer, a handsome cock, 'In al the land of crowing nas his peer'. He is the master in some measure of seven hens, and of these the loveliest is the gracious Lady Pertelote, to whom he relates his dream of a

65

strange beast that tried to seize him. Quoting Cato's dictum that dreams have no importance, she suggests that he needs a laxative. He replies that dreams are prophecies and gives two examples, then reminds her of St. Kenelm, young Scipio Africanus, Daniel, Joseph, Croesus and Andromache. That night a lurking fox asks Chanticleer to sing. The cock shuts his eyes—and the fox grabs him. The hens lament, the widow, her two daughters, the whole farmyard, begin chasing the fox. Chanticleer calls on the fox to shout insults at the pursuers, and as soon as the fox opens his mouth, the cock escapes and flies into a tree. *The Nun's Priest's Tale*

CHICHEVACHE: A lean cow: her diet consists only of patient wives, so she has little to eat. Chaucer's *Envoy* to *The Clerk's Tale*

COLLE: A dog, belonging to the widow, who joins in the chase after the fox which carries away Chanticleer. *The Nun's Priest's Tale*

CROWE: Phoebus keeps this white crow, teaches it speech and mimicry. It reveals to Phoebus his wife's infidelity, and he in fury kills her. In remorse he tears out the crow's white feathers, turning it black, takes away its power of speech and flings it to the Devil. *The Manciple's Tale*

DAUN RUSSELL: The 'col-fox' that breaks into the farmyard and flatters Chanticleer into showing he can sing as well as his father could. When the cock shuts his eyes to sing, the fox seizes him by the throat and runs away, pursued by all the farm animals. But when the fox opens his mouth to shout insults at his pursuers, the cock escapes into a tree. *The Nun's Priest's Tale*

DEXTRER: The war-horse of Sir Thopas. The word comes from the fact that the squire rides his own horse, and leads his master's horse on his *right* hand. *The Tale of Sir Thopas*

GERLAND: Garland, another dog owned by the widow, who joins in the chase after the fox carrying away Chanticleer. *The Nun's Priest's Tale*

MALLE: Moll, a sheep owned by the widow. *The Nun's Priest's Tale*

MINOTAUR: Pasiphaë, the wife of Minos, King of Crete, became enamoured of a white bull and gave birth to this monster, half-man, half-bull, which lived in a labyrinth until Theseus destroyed it. The Wife of Bath refers to it as 'a grisly thyng—Of hire horrible lust and hir lyking'. *The Wife of Bath's Prologue;* also mentioned in *The Knight's Tale*

NESSUS: The centaur who threatened violence to Dejanira. Her husband, Hercules, then mortally wounded Nessus with a poisoned arrow. The centaur gave his tunic, stained with blood by then poisoned, to Dejanira, who later sent it to Hercules, who suffered violent pain and death as a result. *The Monk's Tale*

PEGASEE: Pegasus, the winged horse, was given to Bellerophon to help him to conquer the Chimaera. Gawain's steed of brass is said to be 'lyk the Pegasee'. *The Squire's Tale*

PERTELOTE: Chanticleer's favourite of the seven hens in the farmyard. Concerned at the groans he makes in his sleep, she listens to his account of his dream and suggests a laxative. He counters her reference to Cato's claim that dreams have no meaning with a list of famous dreamers. She is as practical and sensible as Chanticleer is vain and foolish. *The Nun's Priest's Tale*

POILEYS, POILLEYS COURSER: A horse from Apulia with which Gawain's steed of brass is compared. *The Squire's Tale*

RUSSELL: *see* Daun Russell

SCOT: On the pilgrimage, the Reeve rides on a sturdy horse 'That was al pomely grey, and highte Scot'. *The Prologue*

The horse that with two others gets stuck with a farmcart in a muddy lane. After shouting to the Devil, the carter gets them moving. *The Friar's Tale*

TALBOT: One of the widow's dogs. He joins in the chase after the fox which carries off Chanticleer. *The Nun's Priest's Tale*

The Characters – Tale by Tale

N.B. For the significance of the line references, see the author's Introduction.

The Canterbury Tales

(Group A)

THE PROLOGUE

The Knight's Tale

(Group A)

		Line
Adoun	(1366)	2224
Amphioun	(688)	1546
Antonius	(1174)	2032
Arcita	(155)	1013
Argus	(532)	1390
Athalantes	(1212)	2070
Attheon	(1445)	2303
Cadme	(688)	1546
Calistopee	(1198)	2056
Campaneus	(74)	932
Circes	(1086)	1944
Citherea	(1357)	2215
Creon	(80)	938
Cresus	(1088)	1946
Dane	(1206)	2064
Diane	(824)	1682
Egeus	(1890)	2838
Emelye	(12)	871
Emetreus	(1298)	2156
Ercules	(1085)	1943
Julius	(1173)	2031
Juno	(471)	1329
Jupiter	(1584)	2442
Lucina	(1227)	2085
Mars	(117)	975
Medea	(1086)	1944
Meleagre	(1213)	2071
Mercurye	(527)	1385
Minotaur	(122)	980
Narcisus	(1083)	1941
Nero	(1174)	2032
Palamon	(156)	1014
Penneus Doghter	(1206)	2064
Perotheus	(333)	1191
Phebus	(635)	1493
Philostrate	(570)	1428
Pluto	(1224)	2082
Salamon	(1084)	1942
Saturne	(470)	1328
Stace	(1436)	2294

Theseus	(2)	860
Turnus	(1087)	1945
Venus	(1046)	1904
Vulcanus	(1364)	2222
Ypolita	(113)	971

The Miller's Prologue and Tale

PROLOGUE

		Line
Pilate	(16)	3124

TALE

Absolon	(127)	3313
Alison	(180)	3366
Benedight, Seinte	(297)	3483
Catoun	(41)	3227
Gerveys	(575)	3761
John the Carpenter	(3)	3189
Nicholas	(13)	3199
Nowelis	(632)	3818
Robyn	(280)	3466
Thomas of Kent, Seint	(105)	3291

The Reeve's Prologue and Tale

PROLOGUE

		Line
Osewold the Reve	(6)	3860

TALE

Aleyn	(93)	4013
Bayard	(195)	4115
Cutberd, Seint	(207)	4127

70

The Cook's Prologue and Tale

PROLOGUE

TALE

(Group B)

The Man of Law's Introduction and Tale

INTRODUCTION

TALE

The Shipman's Prologue and Tale

PROLOGUE

TALE

The Prioress's Prologue and Tale

PROLOGUE

		Line
Austin, Seint	(7)	1631
Moises	(16)	1658

TALE

		Line
Clergeon	(51)	1693
Herodes	(122)	1764
Hugh of Lincoln	(232)	1874
Jew	(118)	1760
Newe Rachel	(175)	1817
Nicholas, Seinte	(62)	1874
Provost	(164)	1806
Sathanas	(106)	1748
Widwe	(57)	1699

Chaucer's *Tale of Sir Thopas*

		Line
Beves	(188)	2089
Dextrer	(202)	2103
Gy	(188)	2089
Horn Childe	(187)	2088
Lybeux, sir	(189)	2090
Olifaunt, sir	(97)	1998
Percyvell, sir	(205)	2106
Pleyndamour	(189)	2090
Thopas, sir	(6)	1907
Ypotys	(187)	2088

Chaucer's *Tale of Melibee*

	Line
Catoun	2405
Jhesus Syrak	2235

	Line
Judas Machabeus	2848
Judith	2289
Melibeus	2157
Olofernes	2289
Ovide	2166
Pamphilles	2746
Piers Alfonce	2756
Prudence	2157
Salomon	2186
Senek	2317
Sophie	2157
Tullius	2366

The Monk's Prologue and Tale

PROLOGUE

		Line
Godelief	(6)	3084

TALE

		Line
Acheleous	(116)	3296
Adam	(17)	3197
Alisaundre	(641)	3821
Antheus	(118)	3298
Antiochus	(584)	3765
Arpies	(110)	3290
Aurelian	(371)	3551
Balthasar	(193)	3373
Brutus Cassius	(707)	3887
Busirus	(113)	3293
Cenobia	(257)	3437
Cerberus	(112)	3292
Cresus	(737)	3917
Dalida	(73)	3253
Daniel	(164)	3344
Dant	(471)	3651
Dianira	(130)	3310
Eliachim	(576)	3756

72

Ercules	(105)	3285	Colle	(563)	4573
Hugelyn	(417)	3597	Cresus	(318)	4328
Judith	(581)	3761	Daniel	(308)	4318
Julius	(683)	3863	Daun Russell	(514)	4524
Nabugodonosor	(155)	3335	Ector	(322)	4331
Nero	(473)	3653	Gaufred	(527)	4537
Nessus	(318)	3318	Genelloun	(407)	4417
Nichanore	(601)	3781	Gerland	(563)	4573
Odenake	(282)	3462	Hasdrubales wyf	(543)	4553
Oloferne	(561)	3741	Joseph	(310)	4320
Olyver	(397)	3577	Kenelm, Seint	(290)	4300
Petrak	(335)	3515	Macrobes	(303)	4313
Petro Rege de Cipro	(401)	3581	Malkyn	(564)	4574
Petro Rege Ispannie	(385)	3565	Malle	(11)	4021
Phanye	(767)	3948	Nero	(550)	4560
Pompeus	(688)	3870	Norice	(295)	4305
Sampsoun	(25)	3205	Pertelote	(50)	4060
Sapor	(330)	3510	Pharao	(313)	4323
Senek	(513)	3691	Pirrus	(537)	4547
Thymothee	(601)	3781	Priam	(538)	4548
Valerius	(729)	3910	Richard, King	(528)	4538
			Scariot	(407)	4417
			Straw, Jakke	(575)	4584
			Synoun	(408)	4418
			Talbot	(563)	4573
			Widwe	(1)	4011

The Nun's Priest's Prologue and Tale

PROLOGUE

		Line
Daun Piers	(26)	3982
Nonnes Preest	(43)	3999

TALE

Achilles	(328)	4338
Andromacha	(321)	4331
Augustyn	(421)	4431
Boece	(422)	4432
Bradwardyn	(422)	4432
Burnel the Asse	(492)	4502
Catoun	(119)	4130
Chauntecleer	(29)	4039
Cipioun	(304)	4314

(Group C)

The Physician's Tale

	Line
Apelles	16
Apius	154
Claudius	153
Jepte	240
Pallas	49
Pigmalion	14
Titus Livius	1
Virginia	213
Virginius	2
Zanzis	16

73

The Pardoner's Tale

(Group D)

The Wife of Bath's Prologue and Tale

PROLOGUE

TALE

The Friar's Tale

Scot	(245)	1543
Somnour	(22)	1321
Virgile	(221)	1519
Yeman	(82)	1380

Janicula	(152)	208
Job	(876)	932
Petrak	(1091)	1147
Walter	(21)	77

ENVOY
| Chichevache | (1132) | 1188 |

The Summoner's Prologue and Tale

PROLOGUE

| | | Line |
| Sathanas | (22) | 1686 |

TALE

Dives	(169)	1877
Felawe	(32)	1740
Frere John	(462)	2171
Fermerer	(151)	1859
Harlot	(46)	1754
Jankin	(580)	2288
Jovinian	(121)	1929
Lazar	(169)	1877
Thomas	(62)	1770

(Group E)

The Clerk's Prologue, Tale and Envoy

PROLOGUE

		Line
Lynyan		34
Petrak		31
Salamon		6

TALE

Countesse of Panik	(534)	590
Erl of Panik	(708)	764
Grisilde	(154)	210

The Merchant's Prologue and Tale

PROLOGUE

| | | Line |
| Thomas of Ynde | (18) | 1230 |

TALE

Abigayl	(125)	1369
Adam	(81)	1325
Assuer	(501)	1745
Constantyn	(566)	1810
Damyan	(528)	1772
Ester	(127)	1371
Januarie	(149)	1393
Jhesus Syrak	(1006)	2250
Judith	(122)	1366
Justinus	(233)	1477
Maius	(408)	1742
Nabal	(126)	1370
Placebo	(232)	1476
Pluto	(983)	2227
Priapus	(790)	2037
Proserpyna	(985)	2229
Rebekka	(119)	1363
Senek	(132)	1376
Theofraste	(50)	1294
Wade	(180)	1424

The Canon's Yeoman's Prologue and Tale

PROLOGUE

		Line
Catoun	(135)	688
Chanoun	(132)	685

TALE

Arnold of the Newe Toun	(875)	1428
Chanoun	(166)	720
Hermes	(881)	1436
Plato	(895)	1448

The Manciple's Prologue and Tale

PROLOGUE

	Line
Bacus	99

TALE

Alisaundre	(122)	226
Amphioun	(12)	116
Crowe	(26)	130
David	(241)	345
Phebus	(1)	105
Phitoun	(5)	109
Plato	(103)	207
Salamon	(240)	344
Senek	(241)	345
Wyf	(35)	139

PART TWO

Who's Who in the Major Poems

The Book of the Duchess
The House of Fame
The Legend of Good Women
The Parliament of Fowls
Troilus and Criseyde

A

Absalon: Absalom, son of David, mentioned in the Balade by the nineteen ladies who dance slowly round a daisy, the flower of Alcestis. He has 'gilte tresses clere'. *The Legend of Good Women*

ACHATES: The chosen companion of Aeneas when he arrives in Libya. *The Legend of Good Women; The House of Fame*

ACHILLES: The son of Pelias and Thetis, he is the bravest of the Greeks in the Trojan War. Betrothed to Polyxena, daughter of Priam, he is slain with Antilochus by ambush in the temple of Apollo, in revenge for the deaths of Hector and Troilus. *The Book of the Duchess*

Pandarus tries to persuade Criseyde to return Troilus's love, quoting the proverb 'To late ywar, quod beaute, whan it paste'. Criseyde replies that he should warn her *against* love, and maintains that if she had loved Troilus or Achilles or Hector or any male creature, he would have held her in reproach. *Troilus and Criseyde;* also mentioned in *The Parliament of Fowls* (*see* Venus)

Achitofel: Achitophel, whose story is found in 2 Samuel 17. He conspired with Absalom against David. When his advice was disregarded he went home and hanged himself. In this poem, the Dreamer says that the Black Knight is as one who confesses without repentance. The Knight replies that if he repented of loving, he would be worse than Achitophel. *The Book of the Duchess*

ADOON: Adonis, the son of Cinyras, King of Cyprus, and Myrrha, so handsome that Aphrodite falls in love with him. He was slain by a wild boar. Troilus appeals to Aphrodite (Venus) to inspire him and to get her father, Zeus, to help him for the love she bore Adonis. *Troilus and Criseyde*

ADRIANE: Ariadne was the daughter of Minos, King of Crete, and Pasiphaë. Ariadne and Phaedra, her sister, hear the groans of the imprisoned Theseus, who is due to be devoured by Minos's monster, the Minotaur. They pity him, and make plans to help him overcome the Minotaur and escape, disguised. Theseus tells Ariadne he has loved her for seven years, and they pledge themselves to marry. After Theseus has killed the Minotaur, he escapes with the sisters to Oenopia where he has 'a frend of his knowynge'. After celebrating their new freedom, they sail to another island, Naxos. But Theseus is unfaithful to Ariadne, now his wife: seeing that Phaedra is the fairer of the sisters, he takes her by the hand one night and 'as a traytour stal his wey' with her. Ariadne wakes at dawn 'And gropeth in the bedde, and fond ryght nought . . . "Allas", quod she, . . . "I am betrayed!" ' She sees Theseus's barge sailing out to sea. *The Legend of Good Women*; also mentioned in *The House of Fame* (*see* Demophon)

AGAMENON: Greek patriarch, King of Mycenae and Argos, a son of Atreus and brother of Menelaus, the husband of Helen. In a great outburst of joy and gratitude Troilus pledges to Pandarus that he will not swear falsely or in any way reveal the love he now shares with Criseyde: he would rather die, he claims, in cruel King Agamemnon's prison. *Troilus and Criseyde*

AGLAWROS: During his long period of despair Troilus appeals to Mercury for help, and mentions the sister of

Herse, Aglaurus, who was turned by Mercury to stone. *Troilus and Criseyde*

Alanus de Insulis: *see* Egle (Animals); also mentioned in *The Parliament of Fowls* (*see* Aleyn)

ALCESTE: Alcestis, daughter of Peleus, the King of Phthia, was the wife of Admetus, King of Pherae in Thessaly. Troilus's sister Cassandra claims that his dream about a boar reveals that Criseyde is now in love with the Greek, Diomede, descended from Meleager, slayer of the Calydonian boar. Troilus declares it is not true: one might as well slander Alcestis, the 'kyndest and the beste', for she gave up her life to save her husband, and only the strength of Hercules (Heracles) could bring her back from the envoy of Hades. *Troilus and Criseyde*

The poet dreams he is in a meadow looking for the daisy. Cupid leads in Alcestis, 'the noble quene Corouned with whit, and clothed al in grene', that is, looking like a daisy. Nineteen ladies, faithful in love, see a daisy there, slowly dance round it and sing a ballade. Alcestis defends the poet-dreamer (Chaucer) against Cupid's accusations that he has been unfair to women. *The Legend of Good Women*

ALCIONE: Alcyone, the wife of King Cëyx. He is drowned in a shipwreck. After she has prayed to Juno for news of him, he appears to Alcyone in a dream and tells her of his death. She 'deyede within the thridde morwe'. *The Book of the Duchess*

Alcipyades: Alcibiades. The Dreamer tells the bereaved Black Knight that he can well believe his late wife to have been the very fairest of women. The Knight replies that all who saw her said so, and even if they had not, though he had all the beauty of the noble Athenian Alcibiades, the strength of Hercules, the worthiness of Alexander the Great, the hardiness of Hector and the wisdom of Minerva, he would ever have loved her, for she was the fairest and the best. *The Book of the Duchess*

ALETE: Alecto, one of the Furies. *Troilus and Criseyde*

Aleyn: Alanus de Insulis, Alain de Lille (*c.* 1128–1202), the author of *De Planctu Naturae*. *The Parliament of Fowls*

Alisaundre: Alexander, *see* Fame

Alisaundre Macedo: Alexander of Macedon, *see* Egle (Animals)

ALMENA: Alcmena was the daughter of Electryon, King of Mycenae. She married her cousin Amphitryon and during his absence was visited by Zeus (Jove) disguised as Amphitryon. From this union was born her son, Hercules (Heracles). After their night of love, Criseyde says to Troilus, 'O nyght, allas! why nyltow over us hove, As longe as whan Almena lay by Jove?' *Troilus and Criseyde*

AMETE: Admetus, King of Pherae in Thessaly and husband of Alcestis. *Troilus and Criseyde*

AMPHIORAX: Amphiaraus, an Argive hero and a seer, who married Eriphyle and took part in the expedition of the Seven against Thebes, knowing all save Adrastus would die. At Thebes he himself was swallowed up in the earth. As Criseyde says to Pandarus, having read the story aloud to her maidens, he 'fil thorugh the ground to helle'. *Troilus and Criseyde*

ANCHISES: *see* Dido; Eneas; Sybile

ANDROGEUS: The son of Minos, King of Crete, he is sent by his father to school in Athens, where he is slain out of malice. Minos comes to avenge his death, and besieges

Alcathoe, the citadel of Megara. Scylla, daughter of Nisus, King of Megara, falls in love with Minos and enables him to take the city. *The Legend of Good Women*

ANNE: Anna, *see* Dido

ANTENOR, ANTHENOR: Antenor, a Trojan warrior, is one of the elders of Troy during the siege, in favour of restoring Helen to the Greeks. Criseyde and Thoas are exchanged for him at Calchas's request. This 'so wys and ek so bold baroun' afterwards becomes a 'traitour to the town of Troye'. *Troilus and Criseyde*

The Black Knight feels that if he were to repent of loving he would be worse than the traitor Antenor, who betrayed Troy by sending the Palladium, a statue of Pallas Athena, to Ulysses. *The Book of the Duchess*

ANTIGONE: A Trojan maiden who is Criseyde's niece, and a close friend. When they are in a garden together, she sings a hymn idealizing love which encourages Criseyde to commit herself to Troilus. *Troilus and Criseyde*

Antonius, Antony: After the death of his wife Fulvia, he married Octavia, the sister of Augustus. He deserted her for Cleopatra, whom he loved so much 'that al the world he sette at no value' (he divorced Octavia in 32 B.C.), and committed suicide after their defeat at the battle of Actium. *The Legend of Good Women*

ANTYLEGYUS: Antilochus, the son of Nestor. He was slain with Achilles by ambush in the temple of Apollo, in revenge for the deaths of Hector and Troilus. *The Book of the Duchess*

APHRODITE: *see* Doughter to Dyone

APOLLO: Geoffrey asks Apollo, god of knowledge and light, to guide 'This lytel laste bok', Book III, which describes the House of Fame, built on a rock of ice. *The House of Fame*

APPOLLO DELPHICUS: *see* Daun Phebus

ARCHYMORIS: Archemorus, stung to death by a holy serpent sent by Jove while his nurse, Hypsipyle, guided the Argive host to the river Langia. He is mentioned by Cassandra. *Troilus and Criseyde*

ARGUS: A monster with a hundred eyes whom Hera, jealous of Io, sent to watch her rival. Hermes slew Argus, and Hera put the eyes in the tail of the peacock, a bird sacred to her. Before she leaves Troy Criseyde tells Troilus she will be back before ten days have passed, as she will cause Calchas, her father, to change his ways and do all she wishes. Troilus feels this man is like Argus, and no blandishments will ever blind him. *Troilus and Criseyde*

Argus: The Dreamer finds the woods so full of trees, vegetation, and animals, that Argus 'the noble countour' could not tell the number. This man is known as Algus, an adaptation of the Arabic surname Al-Khwārizmi of the mathematician Abū 'Abdallāh Muhammad ibn Mūsa. *The Book of the Duchess*

ARGYVE: Argiva, Criseyde's mother. When it is known that in exchange for Antenor Criseyde will go to the Greeks, she cries, 'O Calkas, fader, thyn be al this synne! O moder myn, that cleped were Argyve, Wo worth that day that thow me bere on lyve!' *Troilus and Criseyde*

ASCANIUS: *see* Dido

ATHALANTE: Atalanta, *see* Mayde; Venus

ATHALANTES DOUGHTRES SEVEN: The seven daughters of Atlas, *see* Egle (Animals)

Athalus: Attalus III Philometor, King of Pergamus 138–133 B.C., believed to be the inventor of chess. The Black Knight tells the Dreamer that Fortune played a game of chess with him and took his queen, and added,

'Ful craftier to pley she was than Athalus'. *The Book of the Duchess*

ATHAMANTE: Athamas, King of Orchomenos in Boeotia, married Nephele by order of Hera (Juno). When he married Ino, Hera was angered and drove Athamas mad so that he killed his son Learchus. Rather than see Criseyde go to the Greeks, Troilus pleads that they run away from Troy altogether, but Criseyde replies that they would regret it afterwards. She swears an oath by Athamas that she will remain faithful to him. *Troilus and Criseyde*

ATITERIS: *see* Orpheus

ATROPOS: One of the three Fates, daughter of Night or of Zeus and Themis: Clotho, the youngest, who presided over birth, held the distaff; Lachesis spun out the lives of mortals with her spindle; and Atropos, the eldest, cut the thread of life with her shears. When saying goodbye to Troilus before leaving for the Greek encampment, Criseyde sinks to the ground in a swoon. Troilus thinks she is dead, and draws his sword to kill himself. He bids farewell to Priam, his mother and brothers, and calls upon Atropos to make ready his bier. Then Criseyde recovers. *Troilus and Criseyde*

AURORA: The goddess of the dawn. The Black Knight says he has composed many songs, and that Aurora tells us Pythagoras was the first inventor of 'the art of songe'. *The Book of the Duchess*

B

BACHUS, BACUS: Bacchus, identified with the Greek god, Dionysus, the son of Zeus and Semele. A god of the fertility

87

of nature, he is better known as a god of wine, inspiring music, poetry and revels. Troilus curses him when Criseyde has left Troy. *Troilus and Criseyde; The Parliament of Fowls*

Bernard: St. Bernard of Clairvaux (1091–1153). *The Legend of Good Women*

BIBLIS: Byblis, *see* Venus

BLACK KNIGHT: The poet dreams that when out hunting he follows a puppy into a wood, where he sees a man in black, 'a wonder welfarynge knyght'. This knight, about twenty-four years old, is in great sorrow, for his 'lady bryght', he says, 'is fro me ded and ys agoon'. The Knight identifies himself with sorrow . . . 'I am sorwe and sorwe is I'. In a tirade, he decries the falseness of Fortune, who has taken from him his queen in a game of chess. Later he tells of his lady's beauty and virtues, and of their courtship. The Knight is ever conscious of his loss: 'for be it never so derke Me thinketh I see hir ever mo.' The Dreamer draws out by means of questions the story of both dark despair and happy married life and offers sympathy to the Knight, who ultimately claims that through his wife's death, he has 'lost more than thow wenest'. *The Book of the Duchess*

BRESEYDA, BRIXSEYDE: Briseis, to whom Achilles is unfaithful. One of the poem's classic examples of infidelity. *The House of Fame*

BRET GLASCURION: Glasgerion, *see* Orpheus

Brutus: Junius Brutus, *see* Lucrece

C

CALIOPE: In the proem to Book III, Chaucer appeals to

Calliope, the Muse of epic poetry, to help him to tell 'the gladness Of Troilus, to Venus heryinge'. *Troilus and Criseyde*

Calliope and her eight sisters sing the praises of Fame. *The House of Fame*

CALIPSA: Calypso, *see* Orpheus

CALKAS: Calchas, a Trojan seer, and the father of Criseyde. He has foreknowledge of the fall of Troy, 'And to the Grekes oost ful prycely He stal anon', leaving his daughter behind. She hears all around 'Hire fadres shame, his falsnesse and tresoun'. Calchas brings about the reversal of fortune in the fourth book. He arranges the exchange of prisoners, part of this to be Criseyde for Antenor (another traitor), agreed upon by the parliament of Troy under Priam. Before she leaves Troy, Criseyde tells Troilus that she will enchant her father with words: 'Desir of gold shal so his soule blende That as me lyst, I shal wel make an end.' However, her confidence is not later justified, and the turn of fortune brought about by Calchas becomes the cause of her unfaithfulness. *Troilus and Criseyde*

CALYXTE: Callisto, *see* Venus

CANDACE: *see* Venus

CAPANEUS: One of the Seven against Thebes, mentioned by Cassandra. The proud Capaneus is slain by a thunderbolt. *Troilus and Criseyde*

CASSANDRA, CASSANDRE: Daughter of Priam and Hecuba, and sister of Troilus. She has the gift of prophecy. She interprets Troilus's dream about the boar, first relating some of the 'olde stories' of Diomede's ancestry, and of the sad history of Thebes. Cassandra claims that the boar in Troilus's dream betokens the son of Tydeus, Diomede, who is descended from Meleager, slayer of the Calydonian boar created by Diana. She goes on to tell Troilus that wherever Criseyde is 'This Diomede hire herte hath, and she his . . . For, out of doute, This Diomede is inne, and thow art oute'. *Troilus and Criseyde*

She 'bewayled the destruccioun Of Troye and of Ilyoun'. The Black Knight declares she never suffered such sorrow as he on the day his lady refused his love 'Al outerly'. *The Book of the Duchess*

CERES: A Roman divinity, identified with the Greek Demeter, daughter of Cronos and Rhea and sister of Zeus. She is the goddess of corn and agriculture, mother of Persephone. When Criseyde leaves Troy, Troilus, overwhelmed with grief, 'corseth Ceres, Bacus, and Cipride, His burthe, hymself, his fate, and ek nature, And, save his lady, every creature'. *Troilus and Criseyde;* also mentioned in *The Parliament of Fowls*

Cesar: Caesar, *see* Cleopatre

CESIPHUS: Sisyphus, possibly used for Tityus, who was a giant, son of Ge, slain by Apollo and Artemis for offering violence to their mother Leto. In Hades he was bound on a rock while two vultures tore at his liver. The Black Knight says this man 'may not of more sorwe telle' than of his own. *The Book of the Duchess*

CHIRON: *see* Orpheus

CIBELLA: Cybele, mother of the gods. *The Legend of Good Women*

CIPRIDE, CIPRIS, CYPRIDE: Cypris, Venus, the goddess of love identified with Aphrodite, whose worship was prevalent in Cyprus. (She was often called Cyprian Aphrodite.) Troilus calls on Mars not to hinder him in his grief, for the 'love of Cipris'. As Cypride, Troilus is later to curse her. *Troilus and Criseyde*

The poet beholds Cypride lying in the temple while 'on

knees two yonge folk there cryde To ben here helpe'. *The Parliament of Fowls*

CIRCES: Circe, *see* Orpheus

CITHEREA, CYTHEREA: After the consummation of their love, Troilus turns to Criseyde and praises Love, Charity and Cytherea (Venus or Aphrodite), who was said to have landed on the island of Cythera after her birth in the sea. *Troilus and Criseyde*

Chaucer invokes the help of Cytherea, 'thow blysful lady swete', in the writing of his poem. *The Parliament of Fowls*

Claudian: *see* Josephus

CLEO: Clio, the Muse of history. Chaucer calls upon her to help him as the story moves forward and the 'kalendes bygynne'. *Troilus and Criseyde*

Cleopatre: Cleopatra (68–30 B.C.), eldest daughter of Ptolemy Auletes, King of Egypt. After her father's death in 51 B.C., she was queen in conjunction with Ptolemy her elder brother. He perished in the Alexandrine War, and she reigned nominally with her younger brother, who was murdered in less than four years. By Caesar she had a son, Caesarion. She met Antony in Cicilia, 41 B.C., and they fell in love. The defection of her fleet at the battle of Actium (31 B.C.) hastened the defeat of Antony against Octavian. She retired to Alexandria, spreading a report of her death. Antony stabbed himself. To escape being taken captive to Rome by Octavian, Cleopatra took her own life, 'among the serpents in the pit'. *The Legend of Good Women;* also mentioned in *The Parliament of Fowls* (*see* Venus)

Colatyn: Collatinus, *see* Lucrece

COLLE: *see* Orpheus

Crassus: Marcus Licinius Crassus, *see* Mida

Cresus: Croesus, the last King of Lydia (560–46 B.C.), son of Alyattes. (The story of his dream and death upon a gibbet is in *The Monk's Tale*.) *The House of Fame*

CREUSA: The wife of Aeneas and her young son Iulus are seen escaping from Troy by the poet in his dream. Creusa is lost in the forest and dies. Iulus is the same person as Ascanius. *The House of Fame; The Legend of Good Women*

CRISEYDE: The daughter of Calchas, a Trojan seer. A widow, she has a fine house with a large household. Of medium height, she is beautiful, with fair hair, and clear eyes, is charming, shrewd, generous, kindly and gay. Troilus first sees her in a temple, and at once falls in love. Pandarus carries their relationship further by arranging the exchange of letters. Criseyde, hesitant at first, eventually decides to return Troilus's love, becomes Troilus's 'leche', and accepts him as her 'servaunt' in the courtly love tradition. She goes with Antigone and some of her women to a supper party at Pandarus's house and, when heavy rain prevents them from leaving, Pandarus contrives that she sleeps with Troilus that night: 'out of wo in blisse now they flete.' After the lengthy wooing their love continues for three years, till Fortune cuts short their happiness. The traitor Calchas, who has defected to the Greeks, arranges an exchange of prisoners—including Criseyde for Antenor. At the Greek camp, 'sodeyn' Diomede is quick to take advantage of Criseyde's position and urge his suit. After the tenth day he becomes her lover. Though sincere in her bitter self-reproach, she gives Diomede presents she has had from Troilus, whom she blames for what has happened and soon ceases to mention. Criseyde's faithlessness is presented as a human frailty, that can be forgiven when brought about by the fickleness of Fortune. *Troilus and Criseyde*; also mentioned in *The Legend of Good Women*

Crist: Christ. When Troilus is slain, his freed spirit rises into the eighth sphere of heaven and he condemns 'al oure werk that foloweth so The blynde lust, the which that may nat laste, And sholden al oure herte on heven caste'. Turning from earthly to heavenly love, Chaucer speaks of the Christian faith, 'And to that sothefast Crist, that starf on rode,' he prays 'With al myn herte of mercy'. *Troilus and Criseyde*

CUPIDE: Cupid, in Roman mythology the blind boy-god of love, son of Venus; an adaptation of the Greek Eros, he is described with his 'arwes' and 'bowe' all ready. *The Parliament of Fowls* (*see also* Venus)

In the house of Deiphobus, Criseyde, next to Pandarus at the bedside of the lovesick Troilus, says she will 'Receyven hym fully to my servyse', to the honour of faithfulness and nobility, and 'myn honour with wit and bisynesse Ay kepe'. Pandarus has worked 'this merveille'; he falls on his knees and cries 'Cupid . . . of this mayst glorifie; and Venus thow mayst maken melodie!' *Troilus and Criseyde* (*see also* Doughter to Dyone); also mentioned in *The House of Fame* (*see* Venus)

CYNTHEA: Artemis (Diana), the goddess of the moon, 'hire char-hors overraughte To whirle out of the Leoun, if she myghte'. Though Criseyde promises to return to Troy before the moon has passed out of Leo, she decides to stay with the Greeks instead. *Troilus and Criseyde*

D

Dalida: Delilah, *see* Medea

DANAO: Danaus, *see* Ypermystra

DANE: Daphne, the daughter of the river-god Peneus. She was pursued by Phoebus Apollo and at her own entreaty was changed into a laurel-tree. Troilus asks Phoebus for her love to help him. *Troilus and Criseyde*

DARDANUS: Criseyde, at a window, hears the cry 'Se, Troilus Hath right now put to flighte the Grekes route!', and sees him ride past with all his men to the palace from the Gate of Dardanus, who was the mythical ancestor of the Trojans, a son of Zeus and Electra. *Troilus and Criseyde*

Dares or **Dares Frygius:** A Phrygian priest of Hephaestus among the Trojans. To him is ascribed a work on the destruction of Troy, *De Excidio Trojae*, which Chaucer recommends to his readers, the fall of Troy not being included in his story. *Troilus and Criseyde*

The Black Knight mentions him when referring to the death of Achilles and Antilochus. *The Book of the Duchess;* also mentioned in *The House of Fame* (*see* Josephus)

DAUN PHEBUS or APOLLO DELPHICUS: The father of Criseyde, Calchas 'a gret devyn', has foreknowledge that Troy must be destroyed through the replies of his god, Lord Phoebus or Delphic Apollo, so he steals away to join the Greeks. Apollo, son of Zeus and Leto, was widely worshipped and one of the chief centres was Delphi. He was god of many things, including prophecy. Known as Phoebus 'the bright', he was identified with the sun. *Troilus and Criseyde*

Daunte: Dante Alighieri (1265–1321), the great Italian poet who wrote *La Divina Commedia*, about his journey through Hell, Purgatory and Paradise. For those who wish to read about Hell, Chaucer recommends Dante's writings. *The House of Fame*

DEDALUS: Daedalus, the 'cunning worker', son of Metion and descended from Hephaestus, god of fire and metal-working, who was said to have made statues that could move themselves. In Crete he constructed the labyrinth for Minos. With 'his playes slye' he cannot comfort the Black Knight. *The Book of the Duchess;* also mentioned in *The House of Fame (see Egle)*

DEIPHEBUS: Deiphobus, the valiant son of Priam and favourite brother of Troilus. He helps Criseyde, his friend, in the matter of the false Polyphetes, and aids Pandarus in bringing the sick Troilus to meet Criseyde in his own house. That evening, he and Helen read the letter from Hector, given them by Troilus to gain their counsel. In battle, years later, Deiphobus tears off Diomede's tunic, which is shown in Troy as a token of victory. On the collar is a brooch given to Criseyde by Troilus, who sees it and knows 'His lady was no lenger on to triste'. *Troilus and Criseyde;* also mentioned in *The House of Fame (see Sybile)*

DEMOPHON, DEMOPHOUN: Son of Theseus and Phaedra. Examples of faithlessness follow the story of Aeneas and Dido in the temple of glass, among them one about Demophon, Duke of Athens, who betrayed Phyllis, daughter of the King of Thrace. *The House of Fame;* also mentioned in *The Legend of Good Women (see Phillis),* and *The Book of the Duchess (see Medea)*

DIANE, DYANE: Diana, a Roman goddess, identified with the Greek Artemis. Goddess of chastity and of the chase, she presided over child-birth and was associated with light, particularly the moon. *The Parliament of Fowls*

Troilus, deeply in love with Criseyde, beseeches Diana to help him, 'that this viage be nought to the looth'. *Troilus and Criseyde; see also* Cassandra, Cynthea, Lucina

DIANIRA: Dejanira, to whom Hercules was false. He left her for Iole. *The House of Fame; The Legend of Good Women; The Book of the Duchess*

DIDO: The daughter of a Tyrian king. She has formerly been married to her uncle, Sichaeus, murdered for his wealth by her brother Pygmalion. Dido escapes with some followers to Libya, and there founds Carthage, 'in which she regneth in so gret honour, That she was holden of alle queenes flour, Of gentillesse, of fredom, of beaute'. When Aeneas, fleeing from Troy with his son Ascanius and his father Anchises, reaches Carthage, Dido offers them the utmost hospitality, and soon falls in love with Aeneas. She wants to marry him, but Anna, her sister, opposes this. Dido and Aeneas go hunting; a storm breaks and they shelter in a cave, where they declare their love and are married. Iarbus, the rejected suitor of Dido, is sore of heart. One night Aeneas tells Dido that Mercury has ordered him to sail to Italy. To prevent this, Dido 'seketh halwes and doth sacryfise' and tells Aeneas she is with child; but all is to no avail, 'For on a nyght, slepynge, he let hire lye, And stal awey unto his companye, And as a traytour forth he gan to sayle.' In Italy, Aeneas marries Lavinia. Dido complains bitterly to Anna. Later, she steps upon the sacrificial fire 'And with his swerd she rof hyre to the herte'. *The Legend of Good Women; The House of Fame; The Parliament of Fowls*

DIOMEDE: The son of Tydeus, and leader of the men of Argos and Tiryns in the Trojan War. A courageous, hardy and headstrong warrior, second only to Achilles among the Greeks, he escorts Criseyde back to the Greek camp, is affable, friendly and offers his services. 'This sodeyn Diomede' is a skilled seducer, however, with no need of a Pandarus. He assumes that Criseyde loves some Trojan, and immediately sets out to overcome the opposition. After the tenth day he wins her by deception, in contrast to the honest wooing of Troilus. *Troilus and Criseyde* (*see also* Cassandra)

DITE: Dictys of Crete, reputed to be the author of a work on the Trojan War, to which Chaucer recommends his readers. *Troilus and Criseyde;* also mentioned in *The House of Fame* (*see* Josephus)

DOUGHTER OF THE KYNGE AMETE: Pandarus reads to Troilus from a letter of lament Oenone has written to Troilus's brother, Paris, telling of Phoebus, who invented the art of medicine, could cure every man's pain, but had no remedy for his own sorrow in his love for the daughter of King Admetus. Pandarus then says he can counsel Troilus in his grief, though he cannot always cure his own. *Troilus and Criseyde*

DOUGHTER TO DYONE: In early Greek mythology Dione was probably the supreme goddess, consort of Zeus and by him the mother of Aphrodite or Venus. At the end of Book III Chaucer praises Aphrodite and her son Cupid, the boy-god of love, and also 'Yee sustren nyne', the nine Muses whose abode was by Mount Helicon on the hill Parnassus. *Troilus and Criseyde*

DREAMER: The narrator of the poem, he has lately been plagued by sleeplessness and apathy. One night, to 'drive the night away', he reads 'a romaunce', the story of Cëyx and Halcyone, in which the god of sleep, Morpheus, makes Queen Halcyone sleep. The Dreamer wishes someone would do the same for him—whereupon, he falls into a deep sleep. He dreams that he is woken one May morning by birdsong, goes out on horseback and discovers that the Emperor Octavian is out stag-hunting. A small dog fawns upon him and leads the Dreamer into a wood where, under an oak tree, he sees 'a man in blak'. They talk a long while, but despite the Black Knight's attire, his expressions of grief, his strong hints of loss and the loving reminiscence

97

running through his prolonged monologue, the Dreamer seems not to grasp that the Knight is mourning his lady's death; or, if he does, 'he suppresses this knowledge to afford the Knight the only help in his power—the comfort of pouring his sad story into compassionate ears' (Professor Kittredge). Thus the harsh truth of the Knight's loss is saved until the end of the story: 'She ys ded!' 'Nay!' 'Yis, be my trouthe!' *The Book of the Duchess*

E

ECLYMPASTEYR: In Froissart's *Paradys d'Amours* Enclim-postair is one of the sons of Morpheus, the god of sleep. *The Book of the Duchess*

ECQUO: Echo, *see* Medea

ECTOR: Hector, son of Priam and Hecuba, husband of Andromache, and father of Astyanax, is the leader of the Trojans during the siege of Troy. He is a great warrior, also generous, considerate, and devoted to his family; when Criseyde hears of 'hire fadres shame, his falsnesse and tresoun' in defecting to 'hem of Grece', she goes to Hector and begs his grace. He comforts her, and tells her to live in the city 'in joie'. Later he votes against the plan to exchange her for Antenor. *Troilus and Criseyde*

In his dream, the Dreamer's vast room is covered with paintings, and the glass of the windows tells the story of Troy: of Hector and King Priam, Achilles and Laomedon, and various others. *The Book of the Duchess;* also mentioned in *The Legend of Good Women* and *The House of Fame* (*see* Orpheus)

ECUBA: Hecuba, the wife of Priam and mother of Troilus. *Troilus and Criseyde*

EDIPPUS: Oedipus, *see* Layus

EGEUS: Aegeus, King of Athens. After Minos has conquered Athens, where his son Androgeus has been slain out of malice, he takes vengeance on the Athenians: every third year they must cast lots to decide which of their sons shall be sent to the Minotaur, the monster which Minos keeps in a labyrinth in Crete. Aegeus has to send his son Theseus to the Minotaur, but Ariadne and Phaedra help him. *The Legend of Good Women*

EGISTE(S): Aegyptus, *see* Ypermystra

ELEYNE: Helen of Troy. She is the daughter of Zeus and Leda, sister of Castor and Pollux and Clytemnestra, and the most beautiful of women. She is married to Menelaus, but is carried away by Paris to Troy. The Greek princes resolve to fetch her back; thus begins the Trojan War.

Helen is sympathetic, responsible and gentle, a gracious figure in the high-bred society of Troy, and always kind and helpful to Criseyde. When Pandarus asks Deiphobus for Helen's help, he replies, 'I trowe it be the beste, For she may leden Paris as hire leste'. *Troilus and Criseyde;* also mentioned in *The Parliament of Fowls* (*see* Venus)

Elye: Elijah, *see* Egle (Animals)

ENEAS: Venus tells her son Aeneas to flee from Troy. He takes Anchises, his father, 'on hys bak away, Cryinge, "Allas! and welaway!"' Anchises carries in his hands those gods of the country 'that unbrende were'. *The House of Fame* (*see also* Orpheus *and* Sybile); also mentioned in *Troilus and Criseyde* and *The Legend of Good Women* (*see* Dido)

Ennok: Enoch, *see* Egle (Animals)

EOLUS: Aeolus, god of the winds, is summoned by Lady Fame to the House of Fame. He arrives with Triton, bringing his clarions Clear Laud and Slander, which he blows according to Lady Fame's reactions to the boons requested by the nine companies of suppliants. *The House of Fame*

ERCULES: Hercules, the son of Zeus and Alcmena. The astrological sign Leo is connected with Hercules because he killed the Nemean lion. In the story, the Sun (Phoebus) is in Leo during the end of July and the beginning of August. *Troilus and Criseyde* (*see also* Almena); also mentioned in *The House of Fame* (*see* Dianira *and* Fame)

ERUDICE: Eurydice, a dryad, wife of Orpheus. They were passionately in love, but Eurydice died young. Criseyde sees them together in Elysium, where there is no pain; so in spirit shall she and Troilus be reunited never to part, she claims when she has to go to the Greeks in exchange for Antenor. *Troilus and Criseyde*

ESCAPHILO: A transformation of Ascalaphus, son of Acheron. He told Pluto that Persephone had eaten some pomegranate seeds, and for this reason she could not be entirely released from the Lower World. In revenge she changed Ascalaphus into an owl. Troilus recognises the evil foreboding, for the owl has shrieked after him for two nights. *Troilus and Criseyde*

ESON: Aeson, son of Tyro and Cretheus; father of Jason. His half-brother Pelias usurped the throne of Iolcos in Thessaly, which properly belonged to him, and to Jason after his death. *The Legend of Good Women* (*see also* Medea)

ETHIOCLES: Eteocles, brother of Polynices. Cassandra relates how Eteocles held Thebes wrongfully, having agreed to rule alternately with his brother. Tydeus, one of the Seven against Thebes, lord of the Argives and father of Diomede, went there to claim it for his sworn-brother Polynices. Eteocles sent fifty warriors to capture Tydeus but only one, Hemonydes (Maeon), son of Haemon, returned to him, Tydeus having slain the other forty-nine. Eteocles and Polynices eventually slew each other in a skirmish. *Troilus and Criseyde*

EUROPE: Europa, the daughter of Agenor, King of Tyre. Zeus (Jove) fell in love with her, took the form of a bull and carried her away. She gave birth to Minos. Troilus begs for Jove's help, for love of Europa. *Troilus and Criseyde*

F

FAME: 'Goddess of Renoun or of Fame!' When first seen by the poet-dreamer she is quite small; soon she grows till her feet are on the earth and her head touches the sky. Calliope, the Muse of epic poetry, and her eight sisters sing the praises of Fame. On her shoulders she has the coat-of-arms bearing the names of those 'that hadde large fame: Alexander and Hercules'. *The House of Fame*

FLEXIPPE: Criseyde's niece, friend and companion in Troy. *Troilus and Criseyde*

FLORA: The Dreamer follows a puppy down a flowery green path away from the hunt. He reflects that Flora, the goddess of flowers, and Zephyr, the west wind, must have their dwelling here. *The Book of the Duchess*

FORTUNE: The Knight speaks harshly of Fortune, proclaiming her false and deceitful. In a game of chess she has stolen his queen and left him in despair, longing for death. He will not listen to the Dreamer, who says Socrates despised Fortune. When the Dreamer asks him how and why has he lost his happiness, the Knight forgets Fortune and gives a long, lyrical description of the lady for whom he is in mourning. *The Book of the Duchess*

FUGITYF OF TROY CONTREE: The poet in his dream finds a tablet of brass in the temple of glass telling the story of Virgil's *Aeneid*. The fugitive is Aeneas, who travelled to Italy to the Lavinian strand. *The House of Fame*

FURIES: Cassandra mentions the Furies (snake-headed goddesses of retribution) in her long speech to Troilus. They incited the women of Lemnos to kill all the males except one on that island. *Troilus and Criseyde; see also* Herynes

G

Galyen: In great sorrow at the loss of his wife, the Black Knight says that Galen could not heal him. Galen (*c.* A.D. 129–99), one of the most famous physicians of antiquity, lived at Rome when Marcus Aurelius was in power. *The Book of the Duchess*

GANYMEDE: *see* Egle (Animals)

Gaufride: Geoffrey of Monmouth, *see* Josephus

Geffrey: Chaucer, the discontented poet-dreamer, is picked up in an eagle's claws and carried to the House of Fame. He wonders on the journey 'wher Jov wol me stellifye', and listens in bewilderment to the 'clerkly' eagle giving scientific information on gravity and the way in which sound travels. In the House of Fame he sees a wondrous goddess, and is perplexed by the unjust answers she gives to the nine groups of suppliants asking for fame. (Fame shares the instability of her sister, Fortune.) Geoffrey is taken to a house made of twigs, which whirl about. The house has as many entrances as there are leaves on trees, and is full of noise. The eagle appears, and takes the poet-dreamer inside, as Jove has commanded, to cheer him with 'Unkouthe syghtes and tydynges, To passe with thyn hevyness'. 'Love-tydynges' would seem to be the main object of the journey, but no major revelation is made and the poem is left unfinished. *The House of Fame; see also* Egle (Animals)

Genelloun: The Black Knight says that to repent of loving would make him feel that he was worse than Ganelon, the celebrated traitor of the *Chanson de Roland*. *The Book of the Duchess*

GOD OF LOVE: (Cupid.) In his dream, the poet finds the god angry that he should be worshipping the daisy, for by translating the *Roman de la Rose* and by writing *Troilus and Criseyde* he has expressed heresy against love, 'shewynge how that wemen han don mis'; 'Why noldest thow as wel han seyd goodnesse Of wemen?' he asks. Valerius, Titus Livius (Livy), Claudius Claudianus (author of *De Raptu Proserpinae*), St. Jerome, Ovid and Vincent of Beauvais (in the *Speculum Historiale*) have all written about women, but the poet seems to specialise, unlike them, in the 'draf of storyes, and forgete the corn'. Alcestis now defends the poet-dreamer, saying he has written *The House of Fame, The Book of the Duchess, The Parliament of Fowls* and many other poems, made a prose translation of Boethius, 'And mad the lyf also of Seynt Cecile'. She begs the god of Love 'That ye hym nevere hurte in al his lyve . . . But he shall maken, as ye wol devyse, Of women trewe in lovynge al here lyve'. The god agrees to be just and merciful, and the poet agrees to make 'a gloryous legende Of goode women, maydenes and wyves'. The god praises Alcestis, 'for she taughte of fyn lovynge', and charges the poet to write about her in his work, but to begin with Cleopatra. *The Legend of Good Women*

Gower: John Gower (*c.* 1330–1408), an English poet, friend of Chaucer. 'Moral Gower' wrote *Speculum Meditantis* in French, *Vox Clamantis* in Latin, and *Confessio Amantis* in English. *Troilus and Criseyde*

Guydo de Columpnis: Guido delle Colonne, *see* Josephus

Gyle, Seynt: St. Aegidius, of the 6th or 7th century. *The House of Fame*

H

HEMONYDES; Maeon, son of Haemon, *see* Ethiocles

HERCULES: *see* Venus

Hermes Ballenus: Hermes Belinous, *see* Orpheus

HERYNES: Erinyes, or Furies, 'Nyghtes doughtren thre', 'that endeles compleignen evere in peyne', Megaera, Alecto, and Tisiphone. In the proem of Book IV Chaucer calls upon these to show 'the losse of lyf and love yfeere Of Troilus'. *Troilus and Criseyde; see also* Furies

HESTER: The Black Knight says that his wife had as much gentleness as Esther, wife of the Persian King Ahasuerus, in the Bible. *The Book of the Duchess*

HIERSE: Herse, the sister of Aglaurus, was beloved of Mercury, which caused Pallas Athene to be angry with Aglaurus. Troilus asks Mercury for help for the love of Herse. *Troilus and Criseyde*

HORASTE: One night, in his house, Pandarus tells Criseyde that Troilus is greatly distressed, because a friend has told him Criseyde loves another, Horaste. Criseyde vigorously denies it. *Troilus and Criseyde*

I

IMENEUS: Hymenaeus, or Hymen, the god of marriage, whom Troilus salutes, for after the consummation of his love with Criseyde, 'what to don, for joie unnethe he wiste'. *Troilus and Criseyde;* also mentioned in *The Legend of Good Women* (*see* Philomene)

ISAUDE: Isolde, *see* Venus

ISIPHILE, YSIPHELE: Hypsipyle, the daughter of Thoas, and Queen of Lemnos. One morning, roaming upon the cliffs after a storm, she sees that a ship is coming to shore. It carries Jason and Hercules, who are welcomed and done great honour by Hypsipyle. She at first is attracted to Hercules, who seems steadfast and true, but the two men trick her and eventually Jason, by display of love, deceives her into marrying him. He 'tok of hir substaunce' and 'upon hire begat he children two'. Then the philanderer 'drogh his sayl, and saw hir nevere mo'. However, Hypsipyle remains faithful and dies in sorrow. *The Legend of Good Women; The House of Fame*

IULUS: *see* Creusa

IXION: A Thessalian, King of Lapithae, who married Dia, daughter of Deioneus. Though Zeus favoured him, he angered the god by trying to seduce his wife. For this, in the Lower World, he was chained to a fiery wheel that turned for ever. When Criseyde has departed, Troilus goes to bed in grief, tossing and turning there 'as doth . . . Ixion in helle'. *Troilus and Criseyde*

J

JANUS: The two-headed god of the doorway. He presided over the year and his own month was January. Chaucer sees Pandarus making his way to Criseyde's palace, and calls on Janus to guide him. *Troilus and Criseyde*

JASON: Son of Aeson, he is unfaithful to both Hypsipyle, daughter of Thoas, and Medea, daughter of Aeëtes, King of Colchis. *The House of Fame; The Legend of Good Women* (*see also* Eson; Pelleus)

Joab: *see* Orpheus

Joseph: The narrator (or Dreamer) of the poem needs sleep badly, and 'sodeynly, I nyste how, Such a lust anoon me took to slepe, that ryght upon my book Y fil aslepe'. He dreams a dream which, he is sure, no man could interpret; not Joseph of Egypt who interpreted the dream of Pharaoh, nor Macrobius, the Latin author who commented on the vision of Scipio Africanus Minor. *The Book of the Duchess*

Josephus: Hebrew author of the *Historia Judaeorum*. In the House of Fame, he stands upon a column of lead (the metal of Saturn) and iron (the metal of Mars, god of war) and supports the fame of Jewry. Others stand by him who have written about battles and wonders of the past. On an iron pillar stained with tiger's blood stands Statius, supporting the fame of Thebes, and the name of cruel Achilles. Homer stands on an iron pillar, and with him Dares, and 'Tytus'— Dictys of Crete(?), who wrote about the Trojan War; also Lollius, Guido delle Colonne, and the English Geoffrey of Monmouth. On a pillar of tinned iron stands Virgil, supporting the fame of Aeneas. Next to him on a pillar of copper (the metal of Venus) is Ovid, the clerk of Venus. Lucan, the Latin poet, holds up the fame of Julius Caesar and Pompey on an iron column; Claudian, author of *De Raptu Proserpinae*, stands on a pillar of sulphur (associated with the lower world) and holds up the fame of hell, of Pluto and Proserpina. *The House of Fame*

JOVE: *see* Jupiter

JOVES DOUGHTER: The proem to Book III is an invocation to Venus. She is addressed first as the planet of the third sphere, 'the thridde heven faire!'; then as companion of the sun, 'O sonnes lief'; then as Jove's daughter, the goddess of love. Chaucer asks that she may teach him to describe 'som joye of that is felt in thi servyse'. *Troilus and Criseyde*

JULYAN, SEYNT: *see* Egle (Animals)

JUNO: The female counterpart of Jupiter, primarily the goddess of women. Alcyone prays to her for news of her husband, King Cëyx, who unknown to her has been shipwrecked. Juno sends her messenger to Morpheus, the god of sleep, and bids him take up the body of Cëyx, creep into it and cause it to go to Alcyone and tell her briefly, in Cëyx's own natural voice, how he was drowned. *The Book of the Duchess*

In the poet's dream she runs like a madwoman and calls on Aeolus, god of winds, to blow and drown the whole Trojan nation. *The House of Fame*

JUPITER, JUPPITER: Jupiter or Jove was the Roman king-father of gods and men (as Zeus was for the Greeks), god of light, master of lightning and the thunder-bolt. Pandarus calls upon him 'that maketh the thondre rynge' to make Criseyde forget she is a widow and turn to thoughts of love. *Troilus and Criseyde*

Juvenal: Decimus Junius Juvenalis (*c.* A.D. 60–*c.* 130), the renowned Roman satirical poet who denounced weakness and vice, 'For cloude of errour lat hem nat discerne What best is'. *Troilus and Criseyde*

L

LACHESIS: One of the Fates. She apportioned the thread of life. 'And Troilus shal dwellen forth in pyne Til Lachesis his thred no lenger twyne.' *Troilus and Criseyde*

LAMEADOUN, LAMEDON: Laomedon, King of Troy, who employed Apollo and Poseidon (Phoebus and Neptune) to build the walls of Troy, but refused to pay them when they had done so. Calchas, a Trojan who has defected to the Greeks, says that soon the Greek army will turn Troy to ashes, because Apollo and Poseidon proclaimed, vengefully, that 'the town of Troie shal ben set on-fire'. *Troilus and Criseyde;* also mentioned in *The Book of the Duchess* (*see* Ector)

Lamekes sone Tubal: Tubal-cain, the son of Lamech, according to Genesis 4: 22 was the 'instructor of every artificer in brass and iron'. The Black Knight praises him as master of the art of music. *The Book of the Duchess*

LATYNE: Latinus, with whom Aeneas made a treaty when he arrived in Italy. The poet-dreamer sees this depicted in the temple of glass. *The House of Fame*

LAVYNE: Lavinia, *see* Dido

LAYUS: Laius, King of Thebes, father of Oedipus. His baby son, exposed to die, was rescued by a shepherd, and grew up not knowing his parents. Later, Oedipus slew his father, went on to Thebes, solved the riddle of the Sphinx, became King and married Jocasta, his mother. Criseyde is reading this story to two maidens when Pandarus arrives on the third day of May. *Troilus and Criseyde*

Leonard: St. Leonard was the patron saint of captives. The poet-narrator falls asleep out of weariness, like one who has walked two miles 'to the corseynt Leonard'. *The House of Fame*

LIMOTE: *see* Orpheus

Lollius: Chaucer thought this to be the name of an authority on the Trojan War. *Troilus and Criseyde;* also mentioned in *The House of Fame* (*see* Josephus)

Lucan: Marcus Annaeus Lucanus (A.D. 39–65), a Roman poet, whose chief work is the *Pharsalia*, describing the conflict between Caesar and Pompey. *Troilus and Criseyde;* also mentioned in *The House of Fame* (*see* Josephus)

LUCINA: Before leaving Troy for the Greek encampment, Criseyde swears to Troilus that before Lucina (the moon— hence, another name for Diana) passes out of Aries (the Ram) beyond Leo (the Lion), that is, before the tenth day, she will have returned: 'Er Phebus suster, Lucina the sheene, The Leoun passe out of this Ariete, I wol ben here, withouten any wene.' *Troilus and Criseyde*

Lucrece, Lucresse: Lucretia, daughter of Lucretius, wife of Tarquinius Collatinus. She is 'holden good of alle that evere hire knowe'. Tarquinius Sextus, son of Tarquinius Superbus, agrees to go with him to Rome to see her. So they leave the camp at Ardea and go to the house of Collatinus in Rome, where they find Lucretia quietly working soft wool. She rises at once 'with blysful chere' and kisses her husband. Her beauty and her manner inflame the passion of Sextus. The next day he leaves the camp and goes to the house when night is falling. Everyone has gone to bed. He enters Lucretia's room with drawn sword, 'And as she wok, hire bed she felte presse. "What beste is that, that weyeth thus?" "I am the kynges sone, Tarquinius," ' he answers, warning her that if she shouts he will kill her. Then he ravishes her. Lucretia sends for all her friends, father, mother, and husband, and tells them what has happened. They all justly forgive her, but she will not accept forgiveness; she snatches a knife and kills herself. Junius Brutus tells the people of Rome, and the body of Lucretia is carried through the town. The Tarquins are banished. The tale is told by Livy, and Christ tells the people of Israel that there is no faith so great as that in a woman. *The Legend of Good Women*

The Black Knight declares his wife to have been as good as this 'noble wif'. *The Book of the Duchess*

LUCYFER: As Lucifer, the morning star, 'the dayes messager', begins to rise after their first night of love, Criseyde says to Troilus, 'What me is wo, That day of us moot make disseveraunce!' *Troilus and Criseyde*

LYGURGE: Lycurgus, *see* Phillis

LYNO: Lynceus, *see* Ypermystra

M

Macrobeus, Macrobye: Macrobius, a Latin author and philosopher who flourished about A.D. 400. He preserved the *Somnium Scipionis* of Cicero and added a commentary. *The Parliament of Fowls;* also mentioned in *The Book of the Duchess* (*see* Joseph)

MANES: Diomede tells Criseyde that the folk of Troy are in prison; they cannot escape, and will not receive mercy. The Manes, which means either the gods of retribution, or the departed spirits of slain Trojans, shall be in terror of the Greeks and their vengeance. 'And men shul drede, unto the worldes ende, From hennesforth to ravysshen any queene.' *Troilus and Criseyde*

MARCIA: Marsyas, *see* Orpheus

Marcian: Martianus Mineus Felix Capella, a 5th-century satirist, who wrote *De Nuptiis Philologiae et Mercurii. The House of Fame; see also* Egle (Animals)

MARS: The god of war, later identified with the Greek Ares and regarded as the son of Juno (Hera). His son was Quirinus, identified by the Romans with Romulus. In reply to Criseyde's hesitation over committing herself to Troilus, Pandarus calls upon Mars and upon the three Furies to prevent him ever leaving his house (alive) if he meant her any harm, for it seems that both he and Troilus will die. In the proem to Book IV, Chaucer asks Mars to help him to finish 'this ilke ferthe book'. *Troilus and Criseyde*

Massynisse: Masinissa, King of Numidia. He was visited by Scipio Africanus Minor in 150 B.C. *The Parliament of Fowls*

MAYDE: Atalanta, the maiden of Arcadia who was very fleet of foot. Cassandra relates how Atalanta, 'oon of this world the beste ypreysed', is given the head of a huge boar slain by Meleager, lord of Calydon. *Troilus and Criseyde;* also mentioned in *The Parliament of Fowls* (*see* Venus)

MEDEA: She is the daughter of Aeëtes, King of Colchis. Jason comes to Colchis for his attempt to win the golden fleece. Aeëtes welcomes him, and Medea becomes enamoured of him. She offers to help him through all the dangers of the trial. She agrees to marry him if he will take the oath 'upon the goddes' that he 'ne sholde nevere hire false, nyght ne day, To ben hire husbonde while he lyve may'. The next day he wins the conflict, and the fleece. They go to Thessaly, where Jason later deserts Medea and their two young children—her reward for fidelity and kindness. (Later, he marries Creusa, the daughter of King Creon.) Medea wonders sorrowfully: 'Whi lykede me thy yelwe her to se More than the boundes of myn honeste?' She reflects that had he died in his adventure, much faithlessness would have died with him. *The Legend of Good Women*

The Dreamer warns the Black Knight that even if he lost twelve of his men to Fortune in a chess game, murdering himself would condemn him as justly as Medea was condemned for killing the two children she had had by Jason when he deserted her; as Phyllis, who hanged herself for Demophon 'for he had broke his terme day To come to hir,' as Dido, Queen of Carthage, who slew herself because Aeneas was false; as Echo, who died because Narcissus 'nolde nat love hir'; and Samson, 'that slough hymself with a piler' because of Delilah. *The Book of the Duchess*

By magic, Medea restored Aeson, Jason's father, to youth. *The House of Fame*

MEGERA: Megaera, *see* Herynes

MELEAGRE: Meleager, son of Oeneus. Cassandra relates

that he hunted and slew the Calydonian boar, then gave the head to Atalanta. This angered his uncles, who tried to take it from her, so he killed them. Cassandra hints at how Meleager died. *Troilus and Criseyde*

MERCURIE, MERCURYE: Mercury, a Roman divinity, is identified with the Greek god Hermes, son of Zeus and Maia. Troilus, in his time of emotional distress, appeals for his help for the god's love of Herse. *Troilus and Criseyde;* also mentioned in *The House of Fame* and *The Legend of Good Women* (*see* Dido)

MESSAGER: When Alcyone prays to Juno for news of her husband Cëyx, Juno sends her messenger to Morpheus to fetch the body of this shipwrecked, drowned king. *The Book of the Duchess*

MESSENUS: Misenus, *see* Orpheus

MIDA: After Troilus and Criseyde have exchanged rings in sport, Chaucer comments that those who despise the service of love should be given ears as long as those of the covetous Midas, King of Phrygia, who was given ass's ears by Apollo; or should be made to suffer like Marcus Crassus, defeated by the Parthian King Orodes, who had molten gold poured into his mouth. This would 'techen hem that they ben in the vice, And loveres nought, although they hold hem nyce'. *Troilus and Criseyde*

MINOS: *see* Adriane; Androgeus

MIRRA: Myrrha, daughter of Cinyras, King of Cyprus, was inspired by Aphrodite with unnatural love for her father for refusing to honour the goddess. When Cinyras discovered this disobedience he tried to kill Myrrha, who was changed into a myrtle plant (from which Adonis was born) and wept bitterly. Yet her tears were not so bitter as those which Troilus and Criseyde shed when they know they must be parted. *Troilus and Criseyde*

MODER OF ROMULUS: *see* Venus

MONESTEO: Mnestheus, a Trojan hero, who fails to save Antenor from capture by the Greeks. *Troilus and Criseyde*

MORPHEUS: The god of sleep, who is asleep in a cave with his son Eclympasteyr, 'that slep and dide noon other werk', when Juno's messenger arrives. They follow her bidding, to take the drowned body of Cëyx to his wife Alcyone, so that he can tell her of his death as in a dream. *The Book of the Duchess*

MYNERVA: The Roman goddess of wisdom and of art and trades, identified with the Greek Athene. Pandarus, begging Criseyde to cast off her widow's clothes and think of love, knows that by Minerva, Jupiter and Venus, Criseyde lives 'withouten paramours'. *Troilus and Criseyde*

MYNOS: Minos, a judge of the dead, appointed to this position because of his righteous conduct on earth. *Troilus and Criseyde*

Minos, King of Crete, *see* Adriane; Androgeus

N

NARCISUS: Narcissus, *see* Medea

Naso: *see* Ovide

NATURE: The poet in his dream admires Nature, 'the vicaire of the almyghty Lord', here personified as the creative force, in harmony with God's plan of creation. Nature appears in the garden where the birds have congregated, and governs the assembly. *The Parliament of Fowls*

NEPTUNUS: Neptune, the Roman god of the sea, who is invoked by Pandarus in a last appeal to Criseyde concerning her feeling for Troilus. *Troilus and Criseyde*

NYNUS: Ninus, in myth the husband of Semiramis, and traditional founder of Nineveh. *The Legend of Good Women; see also* Tisbe

NYOBE: She was the daughter of Tantalus, the wife of Amphion. Mother of seven sons and seven daughters, she boasted of her child-bearing achievement to Leto, who had only two children. Apollo and Artemis then killed all her children. Niobe wept till she turned into a stone column. Pandarus tells Troilus that he will never win love if he is to 'walwe and wepe as Nyobe the queene'. *Troilus and Criseyde*

NYSUS: Nisus, *see* Androgeus

NYSUS DOUGHTER: Nisus's daughter Scylla was changed into a sea-bird. Troilus hears it singing, sends for Pandarus, and they walk the city walls 'to loke if they kan sen aught of Criseyde'. *Troilus and Criseyde;* also mentioned in *The Legend of Good Women* (*see* Androgeus)

O

Octovyan, Octovyen: Octavianus, Emperor Augustus (63 B.C.–A.D. 14), the nephew of Julius Caesar and first Roman emperor. *The Legend of Good Women*

The Dreamer hears a horn blow outside and goes to join the hunt, and asks someone with a limer, 'Say, felowe, who shal hunte here?' He is told it is Octavian, the Roman emperor. *The Book of the Duchess*

OENONE: A nymph of Mount Ida, loved by Paris when he is a shepherd. Later he is recognized as Priam's son, deserts Oenone and carries Helen off to Troy. Pandarus asks Troilus if he has seen the letter Oenone wrote to his brother Paris in lament. As Troilus has not, he tells him what it says. *Troilus and Criseyde;* also mentioned in *The House of Fame* and *The Parliament of Fowls* (*see* Venus)

OËTES: Aeëtes, *see* Medea

Olyver: Oliver, friend of Roland, one of the most famous of Charlemagne's knights. Betrayed with Roland by Ganelon. *The Book of the Duchess*

Omer: At the beginning of the work Chaucer tells the reader that he can read about the Trojan War in Homer, for that 'falleth naught to purpos me to telle'. *Troilus and Criseyde;* also mentioned in *The House of Fame* (*see* Josephus)

ORION: Arion, *see* Orpheus

ORPHEUS: He was said to be the son of Oeagrus, King of Thrace, and the Muse Calliope, and was a follower of Dionysus. Renowned for his music on a lyre presented to him by Apollo, he resisted the lure of the Sirens by singing. When his wife Eurydice died, he went to Pluto's domain in Hades to fetch her back, but failed to bring her back to earth. His constancy to her memory so angered the Thracian women that they slew him. His lyre, carried to heaven, was placed among the stars. Bewailing her imminent departure for the Greek camp, Criseyde affirms that though she and Troilus be parted on earth, they will be together in Elysium like Orpheus and Eurydice. *Troilus and Criseyde*

The god of melody cannot drive away the Black Knight's sorrow. *The Book of the Duchess*

One of the inhabitants, which include musicians, magicians and storytellers, of the House of Fame. As well as Orpheus, poet and musician, could be seen Arion the harper; Chiron, the centaur, tutor of Achilles; Glasgerion, a British bard; Atiteris and Pseustis of Athens; Marsyas, the satyr whom Apollo defeated in a musical contest and then flayed; Misenus, trumpeter to Hector and to Aeneas; Joab, who also played the trumpet; Thiodamus, the augur of Thebes. The poet-dreamer sees also Medea, Circe and Calypso: Hermes Belinous, disciple of Hermes Trismegistus; Limote —probably Elymas, the sorcerer mentioned in Acts 13:8; Simon Magus, who used sorcery and bewitched the people of Samaria; and Colle, the juggler. *The House of Fame*

Ovide, Ovyde: Ovid, Publius Ovidius Naso (43 B.C.– A.D. 18), renowned for his *Metamorphoses*, was the favourite Latin poet of the Middle Ages. *Troilus and Criseyde*

The Black Knight tells the Dreamer that nothing can make his sorrows pass, not even Ovid's *Remedia Amoris*. *The Book of the Duchess;* also mentioned in *The House of Fame* and *The Legend of Good Women*

P

PALINURUS: *see* Sybile

PALLAS: The Greek divinity Athene, daughter of Zeus and Metis. She was identified by the Romans with Minerva, goddess of wisdom, industry and war. Criseyde in great uncertainty over her feelings towards Troilus asks Pallas to guide her 'in this dredful cas'. *Troilus and Criseyde*

PAN: The god of shepherds, huntsmen and country folk, protector of flocks and herds, wild beasts and bees, and chief of the satyrs. The Black Knight is so overcome by sorrow that he does not hear the Dreamer's greeting, though Pan, 'god of kynde' (nature), 'were for hys sorwes never so wroth'. *The Book of the Duchess*

PANDARUS: Criseyde's uncle, but by no means an old man. Though not successful himself in affairs of the heart ('I hoppe alwey bihinde' in 'loves daunce'), he takes it upon himself to arrange the love affair of Troilus and Criseyde when the latter's father, Calchas, defects to the Greeks. He takes to his niece a letter he has instructed Troilus to write, claims that a man named Polyphetes is intending to make trouble for her again, thus giving Troilus good cause to befriend Criseyde and offer help, and eventually brings the pair physically together with a ploy to make Troilus believe Criseyde loves another, Horaste. But though he is clever and practical as a go-between, he cannot prevent the exchange of Criseyde for Antenor. Zestful and high-spirited, he seems always to be in a hurry. He takes part in athletic sports with Troilus, loves talking, is frequently humorous, using catch-phrases, proverbs and epigrams freely, and is usually very down-to-earth. Though full of 'jolytee' and 'lustinesse', he disregards 'holiness', never runs any personal risk, and seems to contrive his schemes to satisfy his own sense of drama. Good-natured and warm-hearted as he is, he lacks real insight and knows little of love. *Troilus and Criseyde*

PANDION: *see* Philomene

PARCAE: The Fates, the Moirae of the Greeks, *see* Atropos

PARIS: The son of Priam and Hecuba, and brother of Troilus. As a shepherd, he marries Oenone. Later, at an athletic contest held at Priam's court, he is recognised as Priam's son; soon after, he visits Sparta where he meets the beautiful Helen, wife of Menelaus, and carries her off to Troy. This incident gives rise to the Trojan War. *Troilus and Criseyde;* also mentioned in *The Parliament of Fowls* (*see* Venus)

PARTHONOPE: Parthenopaeus, one of the Seven against Thebes, mentioned by Cassandra. He died of wounds. *Troilus and Criseyde*

PELLEUS: Pelias, son of Tyro and Poseidon; King of Thessaly and father of Achilles. The envious Pelias sends his young nephew Jason to win the golden fleece in Colchis, in the hope that he will thereby meet his destruction. *The Legend of Good Women* (*see also* Eson)

PENELOPEE: Penelope, the daughter of Icarius and mother of Telemachus. The faithful wife of Odysseus (Ulysses), she rejected many suitors during her husband's twenty-year absence. Towards the end of the work, Chaucer asks women not to be angry with him for Criseyde's guilt, and if it pleases them, he will write of 'Penelopees trouthe and good Alceste'. *Troilus and Criseyde*

The wife of the Black Knight was as good as Penelope. *The Book of the Duchess*

Pharao: Pharaoh, *see* Joseph

PHEBUSEO: A Trojan hero. *Troilus and Criseyde*

PHEDRA: Phaedra, *see* Adriane

PHETON: Phaeton, the son of Helios, god of the sun. In sorrow Troilus waits for the ten days to pass, by the end of which Criseyde has promised to return. The days and nights grow longer; Troilus feels Phaeton has returned to drive 'his fader carte amys'. *Troilus and Criseyde;* also mentioned in *The House of Fame* (*see* Egle (Animals))

PHILLIS, PHYLISS: Chaucer makes Phyllis the daughter of Lycurgus, legendary King of the Edones, a Thracian people. After the destruction of Troy, Demophon is sailing towards Athens when a storm wrecks his ship. Neptune, Thetis (a Nereid, mother of Achilles), and Triton, a sea god, see that he reaches the shore of Rhodope safely, where Phyllis is queen. She treats him kindly and he, like a fox, follows the false ways of his father Theseus, the betrayer of Ariadne: he promises to marry Phyllis, takes all the goods he can from her, and sails away to prepare for the wedding. Phyllis writes to him in Athens, declaring her love. There is no reply. She realises how false Demophon has been, and, in despair, hangs herself with a cord. *The Legend of Good Women;* also mentioned in *The House of Fame* (*see* Demophon) and *The Book of the Duchess* (*see* Medea)

PHILOMENE: Philomela and Procne are the daughters of Pandion, a legendary King of Athens. Tereus, King of Thrace, kin to cruel Mars, marries Procne (Juno and Hymen do not attend the festival, but the three Furies are there, and the owl, prophet of woe). After five years, Procne yearns to see her sister. Tereus sails to Greece to persuade Pandion to let Philomela come away for a month or two. Tereus greatly admires the beauty and goodness of his sister-in-law. He takes her to Thrace where, after landing, he leads her to a cave and ravishes her. Lest she should cry out his shame, he cuts out her tongue. Tereus tells Procne that her sister is dead, but by the end of the year, Philomela has woven into a tapestry words telling all that Tereus has done, her payment for loving her sister. Her page takes it to Procne, who pretends to go on a pilgrimage to the temple of Bacchus. Instead, she goes to her sister and they console each other. 'Ye may be war of men, if that yow liste.' *The Legend of Good Women*

Pictagoras, Pithagores: Pythagoras, a famous Greek philosopher, born at Samos *c.* 580 B.C. He excelled in mathematical, geometrical, and astronomical science. The Black Knight, deep in sorrow at the loss of his wife, wishes he had the understanding of Pythagoras. He later mentions that Aurora held Pythagoras to be the inventor of the art of song. *The Book of the Duchess*

PIRAMUS, PYRAMUS: *see* Tisbe; Venus

PIRRUS: Pyrrhus, *see* Priam

PLUTO: Son of Cronos and Rhea and god of the Lower World. He married Proserpina. *Troilus and Criseyde;* also mentioned in *The House of Fame* (*see* Josephus)

POLIPHETE: Polyphetes, who may be a Trojan priest. Pandarus tells Criseyde he is about to go to law again and bring her new trouble. Later, at a dinner party at the house of Deiphobus, attended by Helen, Criseyde and her nieces Antigone and Tharbe, Pandarus tells the guests of Polyphetes' villainy. All curse him: 'Anhonged be swich oon, were he my brother!' All promise to be Criseyde's friend, including Troilus, who is lying ill in another room but promises to help her cause. *Troilus and Criseyde*

POLITES: A son of Priam, who fails to save Antenor from capture by the Greeks. *Troilus and Criseyde;* also mentioned in *The House of Fame* (*see* Priam)

POLIXENA, POLIXENE: Polyxena, daughter of Priam and Hecuba, is loved by Achilles. Troilus falls in love with Criseyde 'that fairer was to sene Than evere was Eleyne or Polixene'. *Troilus and Criseyde;* also mentioned in *The Book of the Duchess* (*see* Achilles)

POLYDAMAS: A Trojan hero whose valour fails to save Antenor from capture by the Greeks. *Troilus and Criseyde*

POLYMESTORE: Polymnestor, King of Thracian Chersonesus, who fights at Troy but fails to save Antenor from capture by the Greeks. *Troilus and Criseyde*

POLYMYTE, POLYMYTES: Polynices, son of Oedipus and Jocasta, and one of the Seven against Thebes. Tydeus, the father of Diomede, was one of the heroes on the side of Polynices in the Theban conflict, and Cassandra relates how the brothers Polynices and Eteocles slew each other in a skirmish. *Troilus and Criseyde*

PRIAM: The last King of Troy, son of Laomedon and husband of Hecuba. Troilus, Hector, Paris are among his sons. Though he laments the death of his warriors and the suffering of the people he is kindly to Helen. He presides over the parliament which agrees upon the exchange of prisoners, of which Criseyde and Thoas for Antenor forms a part. *Troilus and Criseyde*

He is pitilessly slain with his son Polites by Pyrrhus, the son of Achilles. *The House of Fame*

PRIAPUS: A god of fertility of gardens and herds, said to be the son of Aphrodite and Dionysus. In his dream the poet sees Priapus in the temple, standing in sovereign place while folk set garlands of fresh flowers on his head. *The Parliament of Fowls*

PROGNE, PROIGNE: Procne, daughter of Pandion, King of Athens. She marries Tereus, King of Thrace. She pines for the company of Philomela, her sister. Their meeting is arranged by Tereus who ravishes Philomela, cuts off her tongue, and declares her to be dead. Finally, Tereus is changed to a hoopoe, Philomela to a nightingale, and Procne to a swallow. On the third day of May even Pandarus feels 'his part of loves shotes keene', and wakes to Procne the swallow's 'sorrowful lay'. *Troilus and Criseyde;* also mentioned in *The Legend of Good Women* (*see* Philomene)

PROSERPYNE: Persephone, the daughter of Zeus and Demeter, identified by Roman mythology with Proserpina.

Made Queen of the Lower World by Pluto, she spends half the year on earth, the remainder in Hades. Troilus says that Criseyde's arrow will never leave his soul, and when he is dead he will dwell in pain with Proserpina lamenting how he and Criseyde are parted. *Troilus and Criseyde;* also mentioned in *The House of Fame* (*see* Josephus)

PSEUSTIS: Presentus(?) *see* Orpheus

Q

QUYRYNE: Quirinus, *see* Mars

R

RIPHEO, SIR: Ripheus, a Trojan hero. *Troilus and Criseyde*

ROBYN: A common name for a shepherd or woodman. 'From haselwode, there joly Robyn pleyd, Shal come al that that thow abidest heere.' Pandarus is with Troilus outside the gates, and says to himself that happiness will come to Troilus out of the wood if it come at all. *Troilus and Criseyde*

ROMULUS: *see* Egle (Animals) *and* Venus

Rowland: Roland, the hero of the *Chanson de Roland*, one of the most famous of Charlemagne's knights. He was betrayed by Ganelon. *The Book of the Duchess*

S

SAMPSOUN: Samson, *see* Medea

SANTIPPE: Santippo, Antipus or Xantipus, King of Frisia, who fails to save Antenor from capture by the Greeks though a truce is made. *Troilus and Criseyde*

SARPEDOUN: Sarpedon, a Trojan, to whose house Pandarus takes Troilus hoping that feasting, music, dancing and fair ladies will drive away his sorrow. But Troilus can never stop thinking of Criseyde, and it is only with the greatest trouble that Pandarus holds him there for a week.

Sarpedon fails to save Antenor from capture by the Greeks. *Troilus and Criseyde*

SATURNE: *see* Josephus

Scipio: *see* Egle (Animals)

Scipioun: Scipio Africanus Minor (*c.* 185–129 B.C.), conqueror of Macedonia; he successfully besieged Carthage. He visited Masinissa, King of Numidia, in 150 B.C. They talked of Scipio the elder Africanus, and the younger dreamed of him at night. The *Somnium Scipionis* of Cicero is part of his *De Re Publica*. The poet is reading this book. He falls asleep and dreams of Scipio, who acts as the Dreamer's guide to the garden. *The Parliament of Fowls;* also mentioned in *The Book of the Duchess* (*see* Joseph)

SEMYRAMIS, SEMYRAMUS: Semiramis, the mythical Queen of Assyria who was believed to have built the walls of Babylon. *The Legend of Good Women;* also mentioned in *The Parliament of Fowls* (*see* Venus)

SEYS: To combat his sleeplessness, the poet reads the story from Ovid's *Metamorphoses* XI of King Cëyx who is shipwrecked, and of his queen, Alcyone, who prays to Juno for news of him. The drowned king appears to her in a dream to tell her of his death. Alcyone dies two days later. *The Book of the Duchess*

SIBILLE: Sibyl, Cassandra, sister of Troilus. *Troilus and Criseyde*

SILLA: Scylla, *see* Venus

Socrates: The Dreamer tries to console the Black Knight to 'have som pitee on your nature' and remember Socrates, the Greek philosopher (469–399 B.C.). 'For he ne counted nat thre strees Of noght that Fortune koude doo'. *The Book of the Duchess*

Stace: Publius Papinius Statius (*c.* A.D. 40–*c.* 96), a Roman poet, author of a *Thebaid* containing an account of the expedition of the Seven against Thebes. *Troilus and Criseyde*

Strode: Ralph Strode (*fl.* 1350–1400), scholastic philosopher and logician. He was a fellow of Merton College, Oxford, before 1360, where John Wycliffe, whose philosophy he opposed, was a colleague. Chaucer dedicated his *Troilus and Criseyde* to Strode and to Gower. *Troilus and Criseyde*

SUSTREN NYNE: Nine sisters, *see* Doughter to Dyone

SYBILE: In the temple of glass, the poet-dreamer sees the Cumaean Sibyl, who takes Aeneas into Hell to see his father, Anchises; he finds also Palinurus, the helmsman of Aeneas' ship, Dido, and Deiphobus, son of Priam; he also sees 'every turment eke in helle'. *The House of Fame*

Symoun Magus: Simon Magus, *see* Orpheus

SYNON: Sinon, who betrayed Troy to the Greeks: 'his chere and his lesynge, Made the hors broght into Troye.' *The House of Fame*

SYTHEO: Sichaeus, *see* Dido

T

TANTALE, TANTALUS: The father of Pelops and Niobe, Tantalus is punished in Hades for his sin of revealing the gods' secrets or stealing their nectar. He is set thirsty and hungry in a pool of water which recedes when he tries to drink, and near fruit trees whose branches are blown out of his reach. The Black Knight says he suffers greater sorrow than Tantalus. *The Book of the Duchess*

Pandarus assures Criseyde that all will be well when she comes to his house for supper, or he would abide 'With Pluto kyng as depe ben in helle As Tantalus!' *Troilus and Criseyde*

Tarquinius: Tarquinius Collatinus, *see* Lucrece

TEREUS: *see* Philomene; Proigne

THARBE: She is Criseyde's niece and friend. *Troilus and Criseyde*

THEODOMAS: Thiodamas, *see* Orpheus

THESEUS: *see* Adriane; Phillis

THESIPHONE: Tisiphone, one of the winged Furies, whose help is invoked by Chaucer 't'endite This woful vers, that wepen as I write'. *Troilus and Criseyde*

THETIS: *see* Phillis

THISBE: *see* Tisbe

Tholome: Ptolemy Auletes, *see* Cleopatre

TICIUS: Tityus, a giant, son of Ge, slain by Apollo and
Artemis for attacking their mother, Leto. Odysseus saw
him bound in the Lower World, where two vultures con-
stantly tore at his liver. Pandarus declares to Troilus that
he may endure so sharp a woe, but he must act and not
despair. *Troilus and Criseyde*

TIDEUS: Tydeus, in Greek mythology the son of Oeneus,
King of Calydon. He marries Deipyle, daughter of Adrastus; their son is Diomede. *Troilus and Criseyde*

TISBE, THISBE: Thisbe, a maiden of Babylon, and Pyramus
fall in love. When their parents forbid them to marry, they exchange vows of love through a chink in a wall, which stands
between their two houses. They agree to meet one night
outside Babylon, under a tree at the tomb of Ninus.
Thisbe comes first, is frightened by a lioness and flees into
a cave, dropping her wimple. The lioness, 'with blody
mouth, of strangelynge of a best', tears the wimple, leaving
it bloodstained. Pyramus arrives, finds the wimple, sees
the footprints of the lioness in the sand, and, concluding
that Thisbe has been devoured, stabs himself with his
sword. Thisbe comes out of the cave and sees Pyramus
'betynge with his heles on the grounde, Al blody'. In grief
she takes his sword, and beside her dead lover, 'to the herte
she hireselven smot'. *The Legend of Good Women;* also mentioned in *The Parliament of Fowls* (*see* Venus)

TITAN: The sun, whom Troilus chides after a night spent
with Criseyde. He claims that men despise the sun for
causing the dawn to rise so early and thus plague lovers.
Troilus and Criseyde

Titus Livius, Tytus Lyvyus: Livy (59 B.C.–A.D. 17), the
famous Roman historian. The Black Knight acclaims his

wife, for she is as good as Penelope and Lucrece, both praised by Livy. *The Book of the Duchess;* also mentioned in *The Legend of Good Women* (*see* Lucrece)

TOAS: Thoas, King of Lemnos, father of Hypsipyle. Thoas, with Criseyde, at the request of Calchas, is brought to the Greeks in exchange for Antenor. *Troilus and Criseyde*

TRISTRAM: *see* Venus

TRITON: A sea-god who arrives with Aeolus at the House of Fame. *The House of Fame*

TROILUS, TROYLUS: A son of Priam, King of Troy, and Hecuba. Troilus is a brave warrior, 'Hector the secounde'. He first sees Criseyde in a temple and falls instantly in love. Timid and inexperienced in such matters, he lacks the confidence to approach her. It is only with considerable help from his friendly adviser Pandarus, Criseyde's uncle, that Criseyde is brought to give herself to Troilus, who expresses his joy in words from Dante's 'Hymn to the Virgin'. For three years he enjoys great happiness, which is brought to an end when Criseyde is obliged to go to the Greek camp as an exchanged prisoner. Prone to succumbing to sorrow, Troilus wishes to die. Though Criseyde promises to return within ten days, the period passes and eventually Troilus has to admit what he has known for some time: that he has lost her for ever, a blow emphatically brought home to him when he sees a brooch, which he had given to Criseyde in remembrance of him, on Diomede's tunic, which Deiphobus has torn off in battle and displays in Troy 'in signe of his victorie'. Troilus is slain by fierce Achilles in battle, rises to the eighth sphere of heaven, and laughs within himself at the grief of those who mourn him on earth. He condemns 'al oure werk that foloweth so The blynde lust, the which they may nat laste, And sholden al oure herte on heven caste'. *Troilus and Criseyde;* also mentioned in *The Parliament of Fowls (see* Venus)

TURNUS: King of the Rutuli. In the temple of glass, the poet-dreamer sees how Aeneas takes the life of Turnus. *The House of Fame*

Tytus: Dictys of Crete(?), *see* Josephus

V

VALENTYNE, SEYNT: A Christian bishop and martyr under the emperor Claudius, traditionally supposed to have been martyred on 14 February, a date which later became associated with lovers and the exchange of love-tokens. The Parliament of Fowls is held 'on seynt Valentynes day, Whan every foul cometh there to chese his make'. *The Parliament of Fowls;* also mentioned in *The Legend of Good Women*

VENUS: The goddess of love, worshipped in Greece as 'goddess of the sky' and 'goddess of all the people'. Troilus asks for Venus's help in winning the love of Criseyde. *Troilus and Criseyde*

The poet dreams that he is in a temple of glass, where he sees Venus 'Naked fletynge in a see', her doves and her blind son Cupid. *The House of Fame*

In his dream the poet sees her disporting with her porter, Riches. 'And on a bed of gold she lay to reste', personifying a corrupted love 'in dispit of Dyane the chaste'. The lovers in her temple are unhappy, the wall paintings 'of many a story' show classical figures, 'al here love, and in what plyt they dyde': Callisto, an Arcadian nymph, who was changed by Zeus into a bear, later slain by Achilles; Atalanta, turned into a lion by Cybele; Semiramis, changed at death into a dove; Candace, an Indian queen of the Alexander romances; Hercules, who died in agony in a poisoned tunic; Byblis, a nymph; Dido who, to escape marriage with Iarbas, took her life on a funeral-pyre; Thisbe and Pyramus, lovers, who took their own lives in tragic error; Tristram, who died in despair—Isolde found her lover dead and died also; Paris, who died of a wound that Oenone refused to heal; Achilles, who died of a wound from Paris when claiming the hand of Polyxena; Helen, a legend of love; Cleopatra who, to escape being carried captive to Rome, took her own life; Troilus, killed by Achilles in battle after Criseyde had left him; Scylla, turned into a monster by her rival in love, Amphitrite; and Rhea Silvia, the mother of Romulus, who was thrown into the Tiber by order of her uncle Amulius. *The Parliament of Fowls*

Virgile: Following a long literary tradition, Chaucer mentions at the end of his poem famous writers of the past. Virgil (70–19 B.C.) the Roman epic poet wrote of Aeneas, his Trojans, and settlement in Italy, in the *Aeneid*. *Troilus and Criseyde;* also mentioned in *The House of Fame*

VULCANO: Vulcan, the Roman god of fire. The poet sees the god, who 'in his face was ful broun', depicted in Venus's temple of glass. *The House of Fame*

W

WADE: On one important evening Criseyde, Antigone, and eight or nine more of her women come to supper at Pandarus's house. After supper they have music and songs, and one of them tells a story about Wade, of whom little is known except that it is said he had a boat called *Guingelot*, and was a warrior. *Troilus and Criseyde*

WILLE: The daughter of Cupid, who tempers the arrowheads in the spring and places them ready, 'some for to sle, and some to wounde and kerve'. *The Parliament of Fowls*

WIRDES: the Fates, *see* Ypermystra, Atropos

Y

YARBAS: Iarbas, the rejected suitor of Dido. *The Legend of Good Women* (*see* Dido); *The Parliament of Fowls* (*see* Venus)

YKARUS: Icarus, *see* Egle (Animals)

YOLE: Iole, for whom Hercules leaves Dejanira. *The House of Fame*

YPERMYSTRA: Hypermnestra. Danaus and Aegyptus are twin brothers. Danaus has fifty daughters, Aegyptus fifty sons. In Chaucer's legend these two change places. Hypermnestra is the youngest daughter of Aegyptus, born with every virtue, for the Fates have ordained that she shall be compassionate, wise and true as steel, Venus has given her 'gret beaute', and Jupiter has blessed her with tenderness, fidelity, dread of disgrace and gifts to preserve her good name as a wife. At this time of year Mars is feeble and Venus has 'repressed . . . his crewel craft', but 'as hevene gan tho turne' Hypermnestra comes under the 'badde aspectes' of Saturn, 'that made hire for to deyen in prisoun'.

Aegyptus agrees that Danaus' favourite son, Lynceus, shall marry Hypermnestra. (At this time consanguinity is no bar to marriage.) The wedding takes place, and Aegyptus's palace is 'Ful . . . of soun of minstralsye, Of songes amorous of maryage'. When night comes, Aegyptus sends for his daughter, tells her she is dearer to him than all the world, but she must do as he says or she shall die 'by hymn that al hath wrought!' He orders her to cut her husband's throat. He has been warned in his dreams that his nephew will kill him, but which nephew he knows not. Hypermnestra, nearly out of her wits, agrees. Bride and bridegroom retire to their bedchamber, but Hypermnestra cannot use the knife: she would rather die an honourable wife for letting him live. She wakes her husband and warns him; he jumps out of the window and runs away. Hypermnestra follows, but is so weak and helpless that her cruel father has her seized, and fettered in prison, where presumably she dies (this legend is left unfinished). *The Legend of Good Women*

Ypocras: The Black Knight says, 'ne hele me may no phisicien', not even Hippocrates, the Greek physician of the 5th century B.C. *The Book of the Duchess*

YPOMEDOUN: Hippomedon, one of the Seven against Thebes mentioned by Cassandra. *Troilus and Criseyde*

YSIPHELE: *see* Isiphile

Z

Zanzis: Zeuxis, apparently the Athenian painter, whom Chaucer wrongly took to be a writer: 'Zanzis, that was ful wys,' wrote that ' "The newe love out chaceth ofte the olde".' Pandarus, distressed to know that Criseyde is to be exchanged as a prisoner for Antenor and go to the Greeks, tries to comfort the unhappy Troilus, and to persuade him to find another woman—a suggestion which is immediately rejected. *Troilus and Criseyde*

ZEPHERUS, ZEPHIRUS: Zephyrus, the west wind, 'Ibrought ayeyn the tendre leves grene'. *Troilus and Criseyde;* also mentioned in *The Book of the Duchess* (*see* Flora)

Animals in Part Two

ANOTHER TERCEL (TERSEL) EGLE: The second male eagle claims, by St. John, that he loves the *formel* better than the first eagle, 'And lenger have served hire in my degre'; he also says that if she should find him false, unkind, a rebel, or jealous, he should be hanged by the neck. *The Parliament of Fowls*

BAYARD: This is the name of the magic horse given to Rinaldo, the son of Aymon, by the Emperor Charlemagne. The name became synonymous with any horse in literature. Troilus with his young knights is in the temple beholding the ladies. He scorns love, but just as Bayard 'horses lawe ... moot endure' so the proudest man might 'Wax sodeynly moost subgit unto love'. *Troilus and Criseyde*

BOR: Troilus dreams of a boar (representing Diomede) with great tusks asleep in the hot sun, and Criseyde holding it in her arms and kissing it. Starting out of his sleep, he cries to Pandarus that now he knows Criseyde has betrayed him. *Troilus and Criseyde*

CERBERUS: The monstrous three-headed dog, born of Typhon and Echidna, who is the watchdog of Hades. Pandarus tries to cheer up Troilus saying, 'To Cerberus yn helle ay be I bounde, Were it for my suster, al thy sorwe, By my wil she sholde al be thyn to-morwe'. *Troilus and Criseyde*

COKKOW, KUKKOW: The cuckoo pushes himself forward on behalf of the worm-eating birds. He is selfish, caring nothing for the eagles. So long as he may have *his* mate, he thinks it quite reasonable for each of the eagles to be single for life. *The Parliament of Fowls*

DOKE: The duck shouts down what is said by the turtle-dove, asking how men can love forever without cause. Love must be returned. The falcon scolds the duck as a churl: 'Out of the donghil cam that word ful right!' His kind, claims the falcon, is so low that he does not know what love is. *The Parliament of Fowls*

EGLE: The poet-dreamer wanders out of the temple of glass, and sees a large, empty field, above which he sees a huge, brightly shining eagle soaring. It swoops down, catches him in its claws, and soars up again. He wonders why this should happen to him for he is neither Enoch (who walked with God), nor Elijah (who went up by a whirlwind into heaven), nor Romulus (who was carried to heaven by Mars) nor Ganymede (who was borne up to heaven by Jupiter and 'mad the goddys botiller'). The eagle tells him he has been sent by Jupiter (as a reward for his devotion to Cupid and Venus, making books and songs in worship of Love) to carry him to the House of Fame. For his diligent writing has left him little time to know people; he lives, in fact, like a hermit. The eagle tells the poet he will hear more tidings of Love's folk in the House of Fame. Then, calling him 'Geoffrey', the eagle talks at length on gravitation and sound waves, and mentions Aristotle and Plato. As he flies higher, the eagle speaks of Alexander of Macedon (who claimed he was carried in a car into the sky by four huge griffins), of Scipio, who in a dream saw every point of hell and earth and paradise; and of Daedalus, whose child Icarus flew so high that the heat of the sun melted his wings, and he fell into the sea and drowned. The eagle also tells of Phaeton, son of Helios, the god of the sun, who, driving his father's chariot madly, burned the Galaxy with fire, and was slain by Jupiter. The poet-dreamer is confused and thinks of Martianus Capella (*fl.* 5th century) who wrote about astronomy, and of the *Anticlaudianus* of Alanus de Insulis, whose descriptions of the heavenly region must surely be true.

The eagle tells the poet-dreamer about the stars made by the gods of bird, fish, beast, man or woman: the Raven, constellation Corvus; Bear, Ursa Major and Ursa Minor; Arion's harp, Lyra; Castor, Pollux, Gemini; Dolphin, Delphinus; the seven daughters of Atlas, the Pleiades.

Exclaiming the name of St. Julian (the patron saint of hospitality), the eagle reaches the House of Fame, where he leaves the poet-dreamer. *The House of Fame*

FENIX OF ARABYE: The only bird of its kind, the Phoenix, after living five hundred years in the Arabian desert, burnt itself to death on a funeral pile. From the ashes arose a new phoenix. The Black Knight says that in his eyes his wife was the solitary phoenix of Araby. *The Book of the Duchess*

FORMEL: The female eagle, who perches on the wrist of Nature. Nature asks her to make her choice of the three male eagles. She asks the goddess of nature to grant her a boon, a year's respite in which to make up her own mind, during which period she would in no way serve Venus or Cupid. Nature agrees, and tells the three male eagles that a year is not so long to wait. *The Parliament of Fowls*

GOOS: The water-fowl choose the goose to speak for them. He says, of the selection of the first eagle by the tercel-falcon, that if she will not love him, he should be allowed to love someone else. *The Parliament of Fowls*

MERLIOUN: The merlin interrupts the cuckoo, calling him

a glutton, the murderer of the hedge-sparrow 'that broughte the forth . . . Lyve thow soleyn, wormes corupcioun!' *The Parliament of Fowls*

MINOTAUR: *see* Adriane

PIROUS: Pyrois, who with three other swift steeds drew the sun's chariot. Troilus, once more with Criseyde for the whole night, complains that they have brought the day too soon. *Troilus and Criseyde*

TERCEL (TERSEL) EGLE: The male eagle. At the debate to decide which of the three male eagles is most worthy to be the mate of the *formel* eagle, the first eagle says, choosing the *formel*, that he 'evere wol hire serve, Do what hire lest, to do me lyve or sterve'. He certainly has the support of Nature, who says that if she were Reason, 'thanne wolde I Conseyle yow the royal tercel take'. *The Parliament of Fowls*

TERCELET (TERSLET) OF THE FAUCOUN: After the 'noyse of foules' has dropped, Nature suggests that one out of each classification of birds should express their verdict. The birds assent. The birds of prey choose the tercel-falcon to speak. He selects the one who is worthiest, highest in degree, and of gentlest blood (the first eagle). *The Parliament of Fowls*

THRIDDE TERCEL EGLE: The third tercel eagle does not boast of long service, and claims that one may serve better in half a year than another who has served many a year. He declares, 'I am hire treweste man As to my dom, and faynest wolde hire ese'. *The Parliament of Fowls*

TURTEL: The seed-eating fowl choose the turtle-dove to speak for them. She begins by saying, 'Nay, God forbede a lovere shulde chaunge!' She does not praise the goose's counsel, but maintains that even if his 'lady' be cold for evermore, the lover should serve her 'til he be ded'. *The Parliament of Fowls*

The Characters – Work by Work

N.B. For the significance of the line references, see the author's Introduction

THE MAJOR POEMS

The House of Fame

I *The Legend of Cleopatra*

II *The Legend of Thisbe*

III *The Legend of Dido*

The Legend of Good Women

The Prologue Text G

Troilus and Criseyde